LEADERSHIP
AT 43000
FEET

LEADERSHIP AT 43000 FEET

Real leaders don't need a title

CHRIS SMITH

For my children, and their children –
and maybe yours

TESTIMONIALS

'The first thing: do nothing. Then: clear the decks for a couple of days and read this book from cover to cover. Wherever you sit in your organisation – Captain, First Officer or Passenger – Chris Smith will open your eyes to what is really going on. Part aviation adventure, part leadership masterclass, what Chris has seen and experienced cannot be ignored. This is the one flight you can't afford to miss. Only one question remains: who will you lend your executive parking space to while you're away?'

Spencer Howson, Broadcaster, Lecturer, Trainer, Advisor

'Chris Smith provides a long overdue, aspirational take on leadership, based on his extraordinary experience as a commercial pilot. He is completely committed to leading in a respectful, considered and meaningful way by deep engagement with your people. A fabulous book at a time when it is truly needed.'

Andrew Griffiths, International Bestselling Business Author, 14 books sold in 65 countries

'This book teaches us what is important not only as leaders but also as human beings. It tells us that respect for the resilience of others and a sincere interest in people are qualities that are required of leaders, not just pilots. This is an excellent book that guides the readers through the message learned from Chris's own experiences in an easy-to-understand way.'

Keiko Nakahama, Ph.D., Aviation Peer Support Education Specialist, Tokyo, Japan

'Mental welfare for pilots is now focused upon in Japan. Capt. Chris developed the first Peer Support Program in Japan in 2017. He is the pioneer. His experience and knowledge is one of the key factors for safety in aviation. We will always seek his help.'

Captain Naohiro Usui, Chief Coordinator of ALPA Japan Pilot Assistance System and NCA Peer Support and Education Program

'In his exploration of *Leadership at 43,000 Feet* Chris Smith challenges traditional notions of leadership, urging readers to delve deeper into its meaning. His unique perspective not only imparts leadership skills but also emphasises the underlying purpose and responsibility of leadership. This book is a delightful invitation to emerging leaders seeking to embrace their unique styles and develop a sense of duty towards others. Chris' insights are invaluable, highlighting the transformative nature of leadership and empowering readers to lead authentically with strength, compassion and purpose. Prepare for a journey that will reshape your understanding of leadership and its profound impact on those under your guidance.'

Elita Huynh, Innovation Manager, Thales Australia

'In the vast expanse of the sky, where the air is thin and the horizon stretches endlessly, leadership takes on a unique dimension. It is in this rarefied atmosphere, at 43,000 feet, that our guide, a seasoned captain, unfolds the profound lessons of leadership that extend far beyond the cockpit. *Leadership at 43,000 Feet* is not merely a handbook for those navigating the skies; it is a timeless guide for anyone charting a course through the complex terrain of life and leadership.

'At the core of this exploration lies a celebration of the power of humility. In a world often dazzled by grandiosity, our author invites us to discover the strength found in humility, emphasising the importance of low egos. The narrative beautifully weaves the essence of being human – the ability to listen, connect, and treat others with the same respect we desire for ourselves. These qualities, often overlooked in the pursuit of success, emerge as the bedrock of genuine leadership.

'The wisdom shared in these pages doesn't shy away from the realities of life. It acknowledges that life isn't risk-free and that, inevitably, people make mistakes. It embraces the human condition, urging leaders to have courage, speak their truth, and take pride in their authenticity. The narrative extends a compassionate hand to the Juliets, Oscars, Michaels, Cynthias, Gabriels, Josephines and Katies of the world – recognising that everyone is grappling with challenges. It encourages leaders to cultivate empathy, to listen without the need to solve every problem, and to approach each person with respect and a spirit of camaraderie. The author emphasises the need to resist overreacting when things go awry, and instead, to engage the team, empower them, and trust in their ability to solve even the most complex problems. Hierarchies, often stumbling blocks in effective leadership, are dismantled in favour of a more egalitarian approach. The call to eliminate the façade of empty platitudes and to connect as human beings, all on the same level, resonates as a refreshing departure from traditional leadership rhetoric.

'This work is a testament to the multifaceted nature of its author – a highly accomplished captain, a management pilot, a counsellor, a parent, a partner in life' – whose diverse experiences are expertly woven into a tapestry that reflects the richness of life. It serves as a reminder that great leaders are, first and foremost, great human beings. They transcend their egos and self-interest, standing as humble servants to those around them, creating environments where individuals can thrive.

'*Leadership at 43,000 Feet* taps into the essence of what it means to lead with authenticity, humility, understanding and courage. It transcends the confines of the cockpit, reaching into the hearts and minds of leaders across all walks of life. As you embark on this journey through the pages ahead, may you find inspiration to soar to new heights in your own leadership and, more importantly, in your journey as a fellow human being.'

Dean Salter, Former CEO, Jetstar Airways

'I have known Chris for almost 20 years and I can honestly say that no-one has had a more profound impact on my professional career than Chris. As a Training and Check Captain, I was ready to embark on my next chapter and through his encouragement, guidance and counsel, I was able to achieve a Masters Degree in Aviation Management. I wrote my thesis paper on Evidence-based Training which then led to a monumental change in the way professional Flight Crews conducted recurrent training within the

Qantas Group of Airlines when I was asked to head up this new training initiative.

'When I first read the title of Chris's book, it certainly struck a chord with me, particularly the *real leaders don't need a title*. This typifies Chris and his pursuit of building up those around him. Leadership, to me, is all about supporting and developing your colleagues to thrive. Chris, through his passion of wanting to see people succeed, has always had a way of identifying people's strengths and working with them to accomplish amazing things, and of course expecting nothing in return. Now that to me is what real leadership is. Chris is highly respected in the aviation field and when he speaks, people listen, because experience is a valuable asset when flying and managing sophisticated aircraft. As a Captain, responsible for hundreds of lives every flight, getting the best out of your team is an essential quality to ensure the safety of the operation and where leadership can't take a back step, particularly in emergency situations.

'I am sure you will thoroughly enjoy reading this book, as Chris shares with you many of his experiences during his wonderful career, not just in aviation but also his life in general. Leadership lessons on the flight deck can be applied to many situations in both business and our personal lives.

'It is my privilege to write this for Chris's first book, the first of many, I am sure.'

Captain James Mitchell, Evidence-based Training Programme Manager, Jetstar Airways

ACKNOWLEDGEMENTS

I've always wanted to write a book, and a book like this. When the time came for me to take an extended break from my work, a career I've treasured always, I knew the moment had arrived, and so I wrote, day after day after pleasurable day. The more I wrote, the more I wanted to. It was truly a highlight of my life.

It became so much more than a reflection of my life and experiences – more a deep appreciation of it all, and a reemergence of memories; a reliving of them. I especially wanted my children to know more about me and that there's been so much to tell; so much has happened along the way, and as any parent will say I'm sure, there's more to us all.

None of us achieve things alone, and certainly not me. This is no soliloquy. I have my own experiences, some of which I've shared in these pages, but these exist with and because of others. So too, we don't know what's coming our way, and that's fortunate. To know wouldn't be living; just living a script. Not knowing provides us with the limitless; from the magnificent to incredibly hard, the unbelievable to the sublime, and naivety to wisdom. We can then use our imagination to shape our futures for the better.

The cast in my screenplay is boundless. All have had an impact; countless small, but others life-giving, priceless, treasured. These are the ones who really know me; how I think, what I do, what I like, through to my favourite colour (very few know I love 70s and R & B music, and lavender, totally.) Thank you. Just thank you. My family and friends who have been there and borne witness to so many wonderful times, fun, real tribulation, and my successes, failures and mistakes – Kerry, Lauren, Tim and Jaime (around whom my adult world revolved, I've done my best kids. Do yours and be proud you did. No-one can ask more than that. Keep learning, believe in yourself, don't let others pull you down, move on when things go awry, don't hold on to any troublesome past, love and have as much fun as you can); my parents (endless support and encouragement) and brothers, to Jenny McGill and Andrew Ogilvie; Murray McCann; to the fantastic friends from all over in this extraordinary industry (for your fun and for looking after me); to those young people from around the world who became part of my extended family, and so many others close to me. Please excuse me if you will as I try not to increase my error count by attempting to name them all.

More recently, there are those who have become wonderful friends and life contributors. Anna Singleton (the 'world's best photographer', Annielyn Images), Andrew Griffiths (invaluable and patient guide for this book), Elita Huynh (for your friendship and fun), Lorenzo and Bella (more family), Jimmy Mitchell (loyalty), Paul Lyons (wonderful life lessons), Naohiro Usui and Dr Keiko Nakahama (who enhanced my life immeasurably) and my 'uni friends' (for taking care of the 'detail'). To the many organisations with whom I have been associated – especially the airlines and aviation companies (which are extraordinary training organisations, and for the camaraderie and unparalleled life), Griffith University and the University of Southern Queensland, and of course Michael Hanrahan and Julia Kuris who guided me through the publishing world. I'll be forever grateful.

CONTENTS

WE CAN'T KEEP GOING LIKE THIS

'If we're going to have children, families, we have an obligation surely to spend at least part of our lives making the world a better place. If not, aren't we being selfish? There is a difference between breeding children and raising them. They didn't ask to be born.'

THANKFULLY, WE'RE CHANGING

It's late. We're flying out of Singapore, heading southeast towards Australia. Settled into the climb, we take a moment to look out, and down, at what we initially thought were city lights – except these are not the lights of a city at all.

We're over the Java Sea, and these are the lights of countless fishing boats, their catch supporting their owner's livelihoods and feeding the literally millions of people who inhabit this part of the world . . . And then I begin to wonder just how long the fish stocks can last; how long can we do things this way? Can we keep going like this? We can't. As I have the good fortune to have this grandstand seat, able to look objectively it all seems so clear, although I know it's not that straightforward. There are lots of moving parts in this thing called life.

There are lots of moving parts in this thing called life.

I'm a very lucky person to be able to work with and meet people from all walks of life, from executives to new hires, individuals and couples of many nationalities and genders, and from our own beautiful country and other parts of the world. I've learned so much from them all and I thank them. What a privilege.

One of the biggest lessons I've learned is that underneath we're all not that different, but we have very different experiences and circumstances that shape us and our views on life. Once those attitudes are established, they're pretty much locked in, and only another significant experience will change them.

One of my professional lives has enabled me to have so many unique experiences, to see and live so much, and another to learn about people and their lives. People are so incredibly interesting – fascinating – in their own environment. No matter what role I've held, it's the human interaction that has given me such satisfaction in life. I'm an optimist, and I love life. There just aren't enough hours in the day or years in our lives for me.

The thing about true leadership is it's not just about 'running' something, or managing others. It's not about management models or the many other concepts designed to 'engage' people, though they do have a place. It's about so much more – so many other wonderful things: setting an example, playing our part in trying to be good people, being good to others, genuinely respecting them, being good to the environment, and making the world better throughout our one go at life, no matter our belief system.

We've also established a narrative that we are somehow something different to or separate from nature, that we can do whatever we want. We're not, and we can't. Where did this come from?

Thankfully, we're changing.

LIFE-CHANGING STORIES

People have honoured me with their stories, and in doing so display that most precious commodity: trust. The learnings are life-changing, and with this book I want to share some of these learnings with you. It's a window into others around us.

Along the way, I'm going to introduce you to some people – people I think you already know. They may be you, or partly you. I expect so. The chapters about characters are based on real experiences people have had, and mine, but do not reference people in particular. Any similarity is coincidental.

This is not a book about learnings from major incidents. We learn a lot from them certainly, but I think we learn more if we really take notice of things that happen every day. Along the way, I include messages of my own. I hope many of those will be of help to you, so let's talk. Let's talk about things that really matter, and about what true success really is. Let's also learn how we can be happier for others, ourselves, and make the world a better place. It can all be done.

I said to each of my children when they were around 20 years old, 'How about I not give you advice any more, but give of my experience.' I remember their smiles. I think (I hope) they felt respected, trusted, acknowledged as individuals, and loved just as they are. 'But I will still give advice if I think you're definitely going down the wrong path with something serious no matter what age you are!' (My fatherly 'out' . . . I secretly think they felt good about that. Safe.)

Join me. Sit and talk with me. On the way, tell me about you. I really want to know.

Let's start.

INTRODUCTION

WHY?

So, you want to be a leader? Captain? CEO? . . . Why?

Why?

We need to ask ourselves this question often, otherwise we may never really be satisfied. Why do we want to be a CEO? A leader? Because we love our industry? Do we want to make the world better? For power? For money?

What is it?

If we don't know, we may well end up spending our lives trying to reach something that doesn't satisfy us when we get there. It happens so often. People move into careers for one reason or another, not really knowing what the result will be or what the career will entail. We often don't really know what awaits us.

It took me quite a while to find out just what it was that really satiated me. I love flying, no question. The other part of me I discovered though is I love working with people, no matter what role I'm in. Why else would I have become a combination of pilot and counsellor? How fortunate I am to have discovered it. I only wish

1

I'd worked it out earlier. Once we do figure out what makes us tick, we can own who we are. And that's freedom.

> Once we do figure out what makes
> us tick, we can own who we are.
> And that's freedom.

What do you value?

Accountants, engineers, builders, business owners, pilots, even many in the helping professions – do they really know what awaits them when they start out? Are they concerned with that? Do engineers think about whether human beings will be *happy* in a certain structure? In some instances, I'd say, yes, but not all. Do pilots think about passenger care when they're gaining their basic licence? Or do they just relish the act of flight in the beginning? Accountants? No doubt they fancy numbers, but the numbers represent people's homes, their children's schooling, their work, their lives. Even medical professionals – do they truly understand what it will be like looking after people for the rest of their lives, or are they initially mainly fascinated with the study of medicine? Lawyers? Sure, some are drawn to human rights, but there are many other reasons to be attracted to law.

I have also learned that I really value having autonomy, to as far as possible do what I want to do as much as I can. I also know that it's not always possible, and that's okay. At least I can aim for close to perfection. Flying got me as close to being self-employed as it's possible to be without being so, while airborne at least. The only caveat to that is the criticality of the job. As with other careers, what we do really matters. We *have to* get it right. It matters so much that

2

virtually everything we do and say is recorded. That's the difference, and it's a big one.

Did who I am stand in the way of a 'traditional' career path from time to time? Yes, but it enhanced my career so much more, and I'm very happy in my own skin. I've had to rebuild my career several times. I've been so far out of my comfort zone, I wondered whether I'd ever be able to recreate it at all – and thank goodness. In so many ways, life started again. I was able to express the real me and be in charge. Had none of those things happened, I could have had a very good but reasonably standard career, held by the safety and security of a well-worn path. I therefore had to largely fashion my own career, and from that – and with the countless people I have been so fortunate to have met and befriended along the way – I write.

We're witnessing the decline of purely commercial leadership. People want more. Much more. And that's not too much to ask.

For now, imagine you're 18 again. What if we did know then the lessons we were going to learn? What if we could apply them from a young age? Imagine . . .

Now I have you thinking about *why* you want to lead, let's dig a bit deeper and find out *what* it takes to be not only a leader, but a *cultural* leader . . . and the world needs those now, more than ever.

PART I

WHAT KIND OF LEADER DO YOU WANT TO BE?

CHAPTER 1

START BY KEEPING YOUR FEET ON THE GROUND

THE TRIATHLON CHAMP

'What an incredible performance!' the reporter exclaimed, as she interviewed the winner of the Noosa Triathlon, one of the world's great sporting events of its kind. As commonly occurs, he was trying to respond through a state of totally expended energy and breathlessness. Still, he was able to think clearly.

'Those times are just amazing. You've got a legion of fans here!' the reporter continued.

With that, he respectfully stopped the discussion going down that path and said, 'No, I'm not the hero here. The real heroes are all the other participants out there. They're working just as hard as me. They've put in just as much work as me. I'm just coming off a higher base.'

Now most certainly this champion had worked incredibly hard to achieve this, but his point was very well made. The rest of the contestants had also put in their maximum effort. They have other lives. They didn't want to be the champion. They just wanted to give it their all, and this is the point he was making. Essentially he was saying that he, of course, should be pulling in good times because this is what he does. He rejected the idea though that he is 'special' because of it. In his mind, others could be where he is if they spent the time doing what he does, and that's all.

> In his mind, others could be where he is if they spent the time doing what he does, and that's all.

He was a humble man.

KEY MESSAGES

- So it is with leaders, or should be. Not everyone wants to be a CEO. A CEO is coming off a higher base.
- Without other participants, there is no champion. Without other employees, there is no CEO.

Let's talk more about the power of humility. It's potent.

CHAPTER 2

BE IN THE TRENCHES: THERE IS NO SUBSTITUTE

THE UNCONTROLLABLE FIRE

It's the 1980s, and approaching Christmas.

It's 9 pm and the old aircraft had levelled out at its cruising level, 17,000 feet, or Flight Level 170 in aviation terminology. Southeast of Townsville, the crew of the freighter aircraft had just completed their necessary tasks, recording the normal flight plan information – speed, time, fuel remaining, estimate for the next reporting point – and had transmitted the required information to Air Traffic Control (ATC). Retrieving their meals from the oven on board located just behind the flight deck, the First Officer settled back into the right-hand seat, and both pilots started consuming their meals – different food for each pilot to guard against incapacitation in case of food poisoning.

The aircraft was a Fokker F-27, a converted, previously 40-seat passenger aircraft on a standard night run south to Brisbane. Built in Holland in the 1960s, this particular aircraft had seen service across many parts of the eastern states, and this aircraft type was well regarded as a strong, reliable workhorse. By today's standards of course it would be seen as very primitive, with none of the advanced automation or navigation equipment found commonly on even small light aircraft these days. Nevertheless, the crews were very proficient at operating these aircraft.

It was also that time of year. Christmas was days away.

The Captain was from Melbourne, so not particularly familiar with the region; the First Officer quite the opposite, a benefit about to be realised.

This old aircraft was noisy inside – a low, loud droning sound. As a result, pilots would have to use noise attenuating headsets all the time, rather than listen to communications through loudspeakers.

Pilots are incredibly proficient; well-trained to manage emergency situations, all the while knowing that the possible scenarios are endless, and rarely pan out exactly as rehearsed. They therefore must be able to adapt.

This particular evening, the airspace south of Townsville was not covered by radar, as it would normally be. Air Traffic Controllers still monitored aircraft in their airspace, recording their progress through their position reports – the crew providing the controller with their current position, and an estimated arrival time at the next. Should they be late at that next position (with a two-minute buffer), the controller will start the process of locating the aircraft. It could be simply that the pilots have been busy with other calculations or tasks, and don't necessarily have a problem.

Then it happened. The right engine stopped. This was a propellor-driven aircraft. The propellor stopped, with the blades moving to a position 90 degrees to the forward direction of flight. This happens by design so they don't create lots of drag (think wind resistance), which will severely reduce the performance of the aircraft.

This just doesn't happen, does it? Well rarely. Very rarely. The initial reaction was certainly one of surprise (the 'startle factor' being the latest technical description). The sound changed. A slight movement of the aircraft. A pilot's instinctive, instant look at the engine instruments confirming the visceral senses. This all took just moments.

Get it right

Then all the training started to work. The first thing: do nothing. Get it right. Understand what is really going on. Agree on it. Be in control. Now act. First, the memory items – those practised countless times. Then the rest, from the book (these days, electronically).

On this night though, something else occurred.

Both pilots' meals are simultaneously and rapidly dropped to the floor behind the pilots' seats. An engine had failed. Start the procedure. This was happening.

Then, the next unexpected event. Before the engine failure items are completed, the fire warning began. A red light and bells ringing.

This wasn't how the script was supposed to go. Usually either an engine failure or a fire would be simulated – not a fire beginning during the engine failure procedure.

Start again. Agree on what is happening. Start the engine fire procedure. Fire the first extinguisher. Wait 30 seconds. There are two fire extinguishers for each engine. The fire should go out after the first. And 30 seconds is a long time to wait. It doesn't go out. Unbelievable. Fire the second extinguisher. Wait 30 seconds. This 30 is longer than the first. We're waiting for that red light to extinguish – 15 seconds – 20. Realisation – it may not. We're using that time to think about what might be. After 30 seconds the light is as red as ever.

Okay. We both know what this means. Get the aircraft on the ground as quickly as possible.

Okay. We both know what this means. Get the aircraft on the ground as quickly as possible.

There are airports around. The first that comes to my mind is Mackay. Local knowledge can be gold. The radio aid frequencies are embedded in my mind – 308 and 112.7. Tune them up. The needles on the old-style navigation aids point to the airport. The two systems agree. Head there now. Tell Air Traffic Control when we can. Is there another airport closer? The large paper charts come out. No electronics here. Where exactly are we in relation to the airports? Work it out – quickly. The Air Traffic Control radar is out of service, remember. They'd normally be able to tell us the closest in an instant just by looking at the radar screen. Not tonight.

Proserpine. It's closer. The plan changes. The navigation aids. Dial them up. We're heading there. Now. Tell ATC.

We've started a slow descent. The remaining engine is operating at the maximum power allowable for continuous running. Still we have to descend. Losing one engine equals not being able to remain at the same altitude. It's okay though. The aircraft can still operate at a safe level, be it a lower one, and in Australia we're fortunate. There are no massively high ranges. Regardless, there are hills, and not too far from the airport. Terrain isn't a problem up here but we still have to descend.

We find we have just a few minutes to think further about our situation. It'll be difficult, but we agree that I'll go back and try to see what I can out the window – if I can get to it.

This is a freight aircraft. It has large containers lined up one after the other inside the cabin, full of all sorts of things – things important to business and important to people. The containers aren't lined up straight down the middle of the aircraft. They're offset slightly to the right so they're accessible from the left. It means they are very close to the right-hand side of the curved cabin wall – about 18 inches (45 centimetres) or so. Unfortunately, that's the side I want to see. The fire is on the right-hand side. I slide down between the containers and the wall and look out the window. It's tight but doable. The once powerful engine had been stilled, ravaged by intense heat; its propellor lifeless. It's an eerie sight in the darkness.

Then I return, quickly, to the flight deck. How far from the airport are we? We read the distance. How low can we descend at this distance?

We're closer still. How low can we descend now? Watch the charts.

ATC is aware of our situation. They know where we're heading. They want an estimate of our arrival time. We're too busy flying. Triage the workload. I give them our distance out, over and over.

'80 miles.' (Nautical miles are used in aviation. A nautical mile is just a bit longer than a statute mile, and quite a bit longer than a kilometre).

Then, '60 miles.' The controller can work out our speed himself and therefore our arrival time. This is not the time for me to be doing it.

My other reason to give ATC our distance? If the worst happened, they would know where to start looking.

Aircraft are incredibly strong. With an uncontrollable fire though, and on this old aircraft, we don't know what it will do to the wing.

Will it burn through? Will it last five hours or five minutes? There is no way of knowing.

Closer to the airport we fly, as fast as we can, descending.

We can turn on the runway lights by radio transmission. They light up. Two welcome strips of lights in the darkness. We fly over the airport and turn. We make our final approach and land. Safety. We turn off the runway to the small country airport terminal. There is a crowd.

The remaining engine is shut down and the associated procedures completed. We shake hands and agree we thought we'd done a good job.

Somewhere late in the flight, the fire had gone out. I think it was when we were over the airport. It's the last I remember of that red light. The fire services from Proserpine township were in attendance. The town was quite a distance from the airport.

Exiting the aircraft, we checked the outside, especially the engine. The propellor was seized tight, unable to be moved at all. We found out later that the cause was the failure of a bearing in an engine section called the propellor reduction gearbox (the engine turns much faster than the propellor). The summation was that the bearing failed, ultimately became extremely hot and caused the fire (the reason the fire warning didn't come on straight away). The engine had ultimately melted inside.

The local airport staff were holding a Christmas party at the airport. They were giving their kids rides on the baggage tugs and trailers up and down the runway. So much for occupational health and safety, but this was the 1980s remember – anything goes. When we turned on the runway lights and they saw the aircraft approaching, they had scampered off the runway.

Having a drink when in uniform is normally not allowed of course. What would passengers think? After this event though, and as we had flown into the middle of their Christmas party, we graciously accepted a beer.

Heroes?

The following day we were flown to Brisbane and headed straight to the manager's office.

'Ah, the heroes of the night,' he said.

He was a very well-respected and likeable man. It's interesting though how words matter. The comment seemed to cement the significance of the event. I'm not sure I wanted that. There are very few heroes in life, I think. Yes, it was a critical situation, but we are entrusted to do our professional job should these things occur. It's just my view. I think we did it well. But I also think we just did our job.

The problem is, once something like that has occurred, you're different. You're the person something happened to – and you don't always want to be *that person*. Different yes, but not necessarily *good* different. You'd rather some things never happen at all.

> The problem is, once something like that has occurred, you're different. You're the person something happened to – and you don't always want to be *that person*.

We had a conversation about the episode, and that was pretty much it.

Back to work then. No being involved in the investigation. No welfare check. No further talking. No discussion with the

Air Traffic Controller. Nothing. That should have happened. There were three of us in this team. I wonder how that fellow was after the event? How did he see things? What can we learn? How is he today? We'll never know.

Another problem arises if we don't attend to these things: it can come back to us later. The 'what ifs' can start. What if we didn't make it? What about my wife and child? They were not set up for life without me. My other children would not have been born. My life would have been cut short. Their lives would have been shattered. The rest of my family, including my parents, would have been devastated.

HUMILITY IS THE HERO

It can happen to anyone. *Anyone.*

The aviation industry has earned its unparalleled safety record through an extraordinary culture of investigation, technology, training, professionalism, experience, research and information sharing. It also maintains a 'never be satisfied' attitude, aiming always for perfection – complete safety – even though it can never be achieved. To do so, for there to be no risk, would mean not flying at all.

Importantly, what differentiates the airline pilot profession from others is the fact that whatever occurs, and whatever actions are taken, the outcomes affect the pilots on board directly as well as passengers. They're in there with them. That of course is a powerful motivator in the sense that it drives professional pilots to perform their duties with incredible diligence as does self-preservation. The rest – safe outcomes – will follow. The fact is that there is a stark difference between managing a situation which will have personal consequences and doing so when there is no direct personal effect, notwithstanding legal and emotional implications for the person conducting the procedure. Surgery and remotely piloted aircraft operations are two that come to mind as examples, without implying any reduction in the criticality of either.

KEY MESSAGE

To actively implant ourselves into business with those for whom we have responsibility or report to us, in situations that, on the surface, don't have direct implications on us, that is, to **make** it so (to have impact on us), is a statement of true leadership and courage. It sends the most powerful of messages that what happens to those people matters to us, that it will affect us too, that we will stand by them to the end, and that we will positively demonstrate it. 'I'm going to make it impact me, too.'

So it is that anything can happen, to anyone, anytime, and it does ... *all* the time.

CHAPTER 3

CREATE OPPORTUNITIES FOR THE UNEXPECTED TO OCCUR – BECAUSE IT ALWAYS DOES

IT'S ABOUT PROBABILITY AND RISK

It was a medium-length flight as far as international flights go; Australia to Japan – nine hours or so. Still, that's a long time, and things can change. The weather enroute was quite good, with just the usual cloud and isolated storms around the equator. That was standard. We could avoid those. Our destination weather was a little ordinary, however – passing rain showers and low cloud. It would depend on our arrival time whether we would arrive amongst those showers. Of course, no-one knew precisely when the showers would be at the airport, nor our exact arrival time. There are infinite variables in this thing we call 'flight'. We just knew that there was a high probability they would be there throughout the evening. Weather forecasting is like that.

There was nothing unusual about any of that though. Aviation systems in reality are very good. Not perfect, but very good. Proven.

18

As all pilots do, we were carrying fuel to cover weather requirements, traffic requirements for busy times, and a little more if Captains deem it necessary. It's a judgement, but that judgement has to be justified. How much is enough and how much is unreasonable? It costs a lot of money to carry unnecessary fuel. The weight of it alone obviously increases the weight of the aircraft, and so it increases the amount of fuel we will burn to carry it. We're a commercial operation. We have to operate safely but with due consideration for costs.

The flight progresses. As it does, options are monitored constantly, no matter the weather. Airports near the route are checked for weather changes and suitability for a landing if one became necessary. As always, a lot of planning and assessment had occurred before the flight departed, but that is based on forecasts, and forecasts must be confirmed and reconfirmed in real time. The most important, of course, is the destination. Forecasts can and do change.

Think of it this way. Fuel is potential energy. On departure, we have a set amount of fuel. It of course reduces as the flight progresses and we burn it. We never have that amount again, and so our options reduce as well. Remember, we've catered for all of that though through our forecasts. It's about probability and risk.

When we know how much fuel we really have approaching arrival, the forecasts turn into reality. It can vary depending on differences in enroute wind direction and strength, or perhaps due to an inability to achieve the desired cruising level. Or maybe Air Traffic Control can't assign the level we want if there is too much traffic there. Flying higher, where it's colder, generally equals using less fuel. There are other factors such as wind direction and strength, but that's the usual basis.

The arrival fuel is monitored closely. It is, after all, a 'forecast' as well – one we make before departure (probability again). The further the flight progresses, the more accurately we ascertain our true arrival fuel. That tells us a lot. What can we do? How long can we hold, waiting our turn to land? If the weather isn't good on our arrival, how many times can we attempt to land before we have to divert to another airport? Do we have enough to fly somewhere else at all? We've done our calculations. We know what our options are. All on the flight deck have agreed.

We make our final approach to land. Still, it's raining and there is a lot of cloud. Aircraft before us are reporting 'becoming visual' quite low to the ground, but still above the lowest level allowable. The visibility is poor.

The aircraft is performing as it should. We are following defined procedures as per our training. Slowly, approaching the runway, the ground starts to appear in our peripheral vision and the lights, turned to bright by ATC, indicating the runway is near, start to emerge through the forward windscreen, noisy wipers working hard. Scanning between the instruments and outside, it becomes clearer – both the runway, and to us that we're about to make a successful approach.

The system works. We land safely.

Was there a risk we may not have succeeded in arriving, that the weather was far worse than expected?

Yes.

Was there a risk that the airports along the way would have become unavailable to us?

Yes.

Was there a risk that a passenger would become seriously ill and we'd be forced to land somewhere else?

Yes.

Yes.

There are always risks.

We could avoid it all, easily. Just don't fly. Don't go anywhere.

Don't live.

There are always risks.
We could avoid it all, easily. Just don't fly.
Don't go anywhere.
Don't live.

I think often pilots around the world lose sight of how good they really are at managing all this. We all do in our chosen professions. We're sometimes just too close to it to see.

KEY MESSAGE

There's risk and there's risk. Risk shouldn't be thought of as bad.

Of course I'm not talking about dangerous, life-threatening risk.

There's a huge potential upside.

Not taking a risk is a potentially very bad thing.

There is a very *high probability* that unexpected good things will happen.

There is a very *low risk* that nothing will occur.

There is a very *high risk* that if we don't take a risk, nothing will change.

21

'WE HAVE A MISSION FOR YOU, SHOULD YOU CHOOSE TO ACCEPT IT . . .'

'Mate, can you give us some idea of what your company wants? We've got the contract, but we've been given no information about their procedures. It's very hard to provide just what they want.' This, from the manager of a global aviation company, allocated a contract to train pilots for an airline – an airline trying to grow. All the contract company could do so far was provide generic training, but while airlines do adopt procedures from the aircraft manufacturers, they adopt some of their own procedures as well. That's understandable, correct, and a good thing if done well. Sometimes local circumstances must be catered for.

This is a highly competitive industry. No company can afford to lose contracts. Consequently the risk for this external provider was that their training product would be seen in a poor light. How could it not? It could ultimately be seen to not be training to the standard required, yet they didn't have all the information they needed. The managers were understandably nervous but in reality were in a difficult position – having to maintain the contract but operating with one hand tied behind their backs.

I think there could have been an ulterior motive. It happens. Why assist a contractor too much when we want to do the work ourselves? That's fair enough too. Supporting our own employees is very important, however far better to do it in an open manner. We must make the ultimate aim clear to our own staff. It might work commercially for a while to play our cards close to our chest, but in the end, we run the risk of a loss of credibility with our own employees.

I volunteered to help the external provider. Unbeknown to me, this would be a massive turning point in my life. The unexpected was about to occur.

Slowly but surely, as they received the additional information they needed, they updated their training with the correct procedures. Their product became better.

'More please.'

'Can you join our meetings?'

Over time, with the assistance of a very mature and open-minded manager, this became part of my job. I was able to build in a small amount of this work with this company – just a bit, but it continued. As you can imagine, my own reputation with this provider was being strengthened, and it was to become evident within my own company as my skillset expanded.

I felt valued, like I was making a real difference. Besides, it was fun, and it suited my personality. I made friends. I like a large dose of autonomy and creativity. Creativity is not limited to artistic pursuits. Building things is key for me.

KEY MESSAGE

Start doing something others value and you'll become known for it. It becomes part of your job.

Then something else happened. My own airline was expanding, to Japan. They needed to recruit and train Japanese pilots. They needed to have them trained by an external provider – again. And I was now known for this . . .

A phone call. I'll never forget the words. 'We have a mission for you, should you choose to accept it . . .', with very appropriate humour. Would I be interested in going to Kuala Lumpur to work with another international company to align their training product with our needs – to train our new Japanese pilots?

I could hardly contain myself: 'My bags are packed. When do I leave?'

. . . and so the next chapter began.

Immediately thereafter: three trips to KL. Three reports to my own company. Sixty adjustments to their training package. High-level strategy meetings with management in KL. Meeting all the new and excited Japanese pilots. Making new friends and business contacts.

Before this, I hadn't had anything to do with Japan. That was all about to change, as was my life, dramatically.

I became very good friends with many of the Japanese pilots. I learned so much about them, and Japan. I learned also that once I demonstrated they could trust me, I'd earned their trust and friendship for life.

'Can I take a photo? . . . You don't understand!'

Upon completing their training in KL, they came to Australia for more. I was assessing their standards. One particular evening, having completed an assessment with a fellow, I invited him to our place for dinner. He accepted.

When we arrived, I literally had not stopped the car in the driveway when he jumped out. I couldn't believe it.

'Can I take a photo? . . . You don't understand!'

He wanted a photo of the house.

It's not a huge house, but much bigger than he is familiar with, and it's old. Another lesson coming my way.

The table conversation wandered about, as good banter does. My interest in people and mental health became a topic. 'You *have* to meet someone,' he insisted, and then continued on, relaying his own story. He had experienced the big three: divorce, loss of career, and an accident which almost claimed his life. It wasn't the accident that nearly took him, but his mental health – he had been knocking on the door of suicide.

The person he insisted I meet was a psychologist, Keiko Nakahama, who was well known for her work in the Japanese aviation industry. He credits her with saving his life. The next time I was in Japan, he arranged for us to meet – no small task, as it was at least an hour by train for her, but she fit it into her busy schedule.

Instantly, we connected, and a friendship and shared vision grew. We would start mental health programs in Japan – peer support groups. It had never been done there. The subject was not overtly discussed or addressed in that part of the world.

My group of friends grew with every visit I made to Japan, along with their loyalty to me. Like attracts like. They were – are – just phenomenal people. It took several years, working with executives, gaining their trust, presenting our wares, demonstrating our credibility, before the first program started.

I had said to the CEO I thought this would take a couple of years to really get going, but I was wrong. It accelerated in the first year, and has never looked back. More people wanted to join the initial group of six. Six became ten, and twelve. Other departments wanted to set up their own version. We gained stature. They would send representatives to Australia to our seminars to learn.

Japanese friends and their families would stay at our home. I stayed with them at their traditional home in Japan.

Ah yes, the 'house' lesson.

How fortunate am I? I stayed at that fellow's mother's house, in a seaside place called Misaki, on the east coast. Large cars can't drive there, the small roads are just so narrow. We stop at the outskirts of town to change to a smaller vehicle, yet we still scraped the fences at times.

What a simply beautiful experience, to stay with friends, sleeping on the floor of a typical local home.

'Can I take a photo? . . . You don't understand!'

WE MAKE OUR OWN LIVES

I have now presented at more Japanese online conferences than I can remember, with a translator allocated to me. Wonderful.

Keiko Nakahama, now Doctor Nakahama, is one of my closest friends.

. . . and the pilot with the 'big three'? He's like family, and his family, like family.

On one occasion, after they'd been staying, we drove them to the airport for their return to Japan. Walking into what felt like an empty house, naturally feeling a bit low, something caught my eye, something different in a photo frame. The photo was an old one of me, one that I never 'see' any more. It had become like wallpaper, not noticeable. But this time it drew me closer. In the lower corner was now another photo – a passport photo – of my friend. It was his way of showing his total loyalty, and belonging. I have never experienced anything like that moment.

My life? It's changed completely, exponentially, for the better. I cannot imagine what life would have been like had I not met them all. From volunteering to finding some of my closest friends and working in Japan. How could that ever happen? You know what? It has nothing to do with luck.

We make our own lives.

From that first step things grew, and grew, and my life has been enriched beyond my wildest dreams.

I read a fascinating article in the *Wall Street Journal*, about 'hot streaks' (breakthroughs, successes) in careers. Northwestern University research had shown that a 'hot streak' usually lasted four or five years, and some people had more than one. It also said that they were more likely in younger people but only because 'not enough people keep plugging away late in their careers'.

One thing is certain, wrote Dashun Wang, who led the study: 'A sure way to prevent a hot streak is to stop producing altogether.'

Me: it has nothing to do with age.

KEY MESSAGES

- If we do what everyone else does, we get what everyone else gets. That might be fine for some. But is it right for you? Do something different. Back yourself. Take a chance.
- Provide someone with something they want, or need, and see what happens.
- Let your staff have a go. Loosen the reigns sometimes and see where it leads them, and you. It's highly likely they'll write you a new, exciting script.
- Big things happen. The unexpected happens. All the time.

The more experience we have dealing with the unexpected, the less surprised or overwhelmed we become. Not only do we become better at handling such events, we often actually start to welcome them.

Take the unexpected, back yourself, be different and have a go. The upside can be more than you can imagine.

There are those for whom the unexpected hardly ever occurs. Why? Because they don't actually do much.

Then again, they aren't leaders like you, are they?

Sometimes when things go wrong, we have no choice but to improvise . . .

CHAPTER 4

STOP. THINK.
WORK IT OUT

**IT WON'T ALL BE IN A MANUAL. SOMEONE HAS TO
TAKE RESPONSIBILITY. LET IT BE YOU.**

In hindsight, and with experience, it was not a good aircraft type endorsement. In fact, it was probably the worst of all my endorsements throughout my career.

I was 21. The aircraft was a Nomad, an Australian-built short take-off and landing aeroplane, and this one was the 'Search Master' model, fitted with advanced radar and electronic surveillance monitoring equipment. This particular aircraft was one of two operated by the Australian Customs Department.

Being 21 is just so young, even though we don't know it at the time. We think we're quite worldly, though there are plenty of people around the world who have had no choice but to grow up too quickly, experiencing things no young person should (or anyone for that matter).

Nevertheless, this is how growth occurs. The years between 18 and 25 I've always termed the 'knockaround' years. This is the time when we've left school, probably left home, know not much about how the world really works, maybe share-house with others, learn that they've been brought up very differently, offend others inadvertently, are offended by others also, make mistakes, and learn.

These are invaluable years.

Sometimes too, if we're lucky, we're given responsibility.

Sadly, drugs are a deadly blight on the world. It's a part of human nature most of us would rather didn't even *exist*: the desire to make money at the expense of others. How utterly tragic that some people are so greedy and ruthless. Then there are others, so desperate for survival that they will do literally anything, even sell themselves for others' pleasure. So many in the world aren't concerned about climate change or any of the other major global problems. They're just trying to feed themselves, today, and it just shouldn't be.

This, though, isn't about the societal scourge. We have to deal with what is. The drug problem is here and we must do something about it

So it is that protectors of our country exist, such as the Customs Department.

It's the early '80s, and Customs are operating these aircraft along the Western Australian coastline, monitoring shipping and other movements. They have their intelligence. They have a lot of knowledge. This mission is to shadow a particular cargo ship, sailing south down the coast. There are several crews, with both pilots and Customs Officers, on a continual 24-hour roster moving down the coast. We'd stay at townships on the way and change crews. Out we would fly, covertly watching this ship, day and night, waiting for a drop off. It could be drugs dropped off the side to be collected, but we're not sure. The 'intel' is there, nevertheless. There are drugs aboard.

I'd had little experience on this aircraft, much the same as most of the other pilots, and the majority of us were quite young.

It's 2 am. We're about 200 nautical miles, or 370 kilometres, off the WA coast, over the Indian Ocean, and we're flying very low. We had special approval to fly to 100 feet by day. This evening we were at about 500. On board are the pilot (these aircraft are 'single pilot' aircraft) and three Customs Officers.

I'm flying under their direction – away from and behind the ship. We've been on patrol for our allotted hours and it's time to return. I make a radio call to what was then called 'Flight Service'. It's a bit like an Air Traffic Control system without being 'controlled'. They provided information and monitored our progress.

The very instant I transmitted, it occurred – and I knew what had happened. The navigation system, a Doppler system, old fashioned by today's standards but the very latest at the time, shut down. Emerging from the deepest recesses of my mind came discussions with my fellow pilots. This is where the real learning takes place. 'Whatever you do, don't transmit on the HF radio with the autopilot engaged, because the Doppler will drop out. We don't know why but it does, and we've all done it!'

Sure enough . . .

Damn . . .

Okay, well Australia is east. We still have our very basic navigation aids on board, but we're too far out and too low to receive those signals. The Nomad is also slow, and we've used the fuel we'd allocated for our surveillance and are returning with the minimum. We need to fly as accurately as we can.

As pilots, we're trained to not show concern. If we do, how will the passengers react?

31

Think . . .

'Hey, Bob,' (not his real name) I said to the Customs agent who was paying close attention to his own radar system. 'Just how good is that radar of yours, really?' I keep it light; fun even.

Bob, rightly very proud of the capability of his system, '*Really* good!' He could see the WA coastline, right there on his dimly lit radar screen with its classic green hue.

Me, 'Bet you can't find Geraldton with it!'

Him, 'Bet I can!'

Me, 'Okay then, how about you give me a heading to fly.'

Him, 'Right! Steer 105.' (degrees)

Geraldton . . . here we come . . .

They never knew we'd lost the navigation system.

Climbing to a higher altitude, as we flew closer to the WA coast we were able to pick up the basic navigation aids.

It's okay. Sometimes we just have to work it out some other way.

WHAT KIND OF LEADER ARE YOU?

There are as many kinds of managers as there are businesses, but they do also fall into two broad categories. There are *managers*, and there are *managers who do a management job*, and they are two very different beings.

There are as many kinds of managers as there are businesses, but they do also fall into two broad categories.

By the book

Those who do a management job follow the book to the letter. They are the ultimate PD (position description) conformers. They will not deviate. If they are required to address an employee about an issue, they will ensure they issue an appropriately worded letter, often drafted not by themselves but by a legal representative or HR. (It's understandable in a litigious society, but in doing so all the time, we're feeding the problem massively and to our own detriment.) That's not managing. It's being a messenger.

They are strongly favoured by executives who don't want to be challenged, who are only comfortable with everyone in a box, who may well be quite successful but still have a high opinion of their own opinion. It's either that, or they're afraid that someone else will shine and progress past them. Sadly, they often don't realise they're holding *themselves* back from greater things. This kind of manager suits them down to the ground, and remember, too often like promotes like, so a certain management culture tends to perpetuate. This kind of manager will also not take a chance . . . unfortunately.

Rewriting the book

Then there's the other kind. This one changes companies, as long as they are allowed. This one fills the requirements of the PD – and more. They are often not 'detail' people. They are often visionaries. They can become frustrated. They may not adhere to their job description absolutely. In fact, over time, they may deviate further, even to the annoyance of their own immediate manager (who is probably in the other category). What's happening is that this person is growing. Their PD is no longer fit for purpose – for *their* purpose. Then again, it may never have been. These people are much more entrepreneurial. This one is a leader, no matter where they are on the org chart.

So often they find that they are being frustrated by mid-level and senior managers, those who are not quite at the top tier – small thinkers nevertheless.

They will take chances. They will back themselves. They may not even know they are upsetting others around them. Though they usually have the untold respect and admiration of the masses.

True entrepreneurial executives really like these people. They are not afraid of them. They embrace them.

KEY MESSAGES

- Think about the word 'manager'. It implies one of two things: firstly, that a person is in charge of others, that they are leading them; or secondly, that they are tending to a particular field or role. In this case, they are not managing. They are an administrator, representative or perhaps a specialist. Sure, we need people who do these tasks. But don't call them managers, please. They are not.
- Get rid of 'stoppers', those in senior or influential positions who put a lid on big and alternative thinkers.
- Take responsibility. Have the courage to back yourself, be non-standard and be criticised, or even laughed at. There's very little downside and huge upside.

It's just too easy an approach to take to match everyone else. It's the 'do what everyone else does so we match their performance' idea – like often occurs in investing. Sure, we have to spread our investments to balance the risk, but if we don't have *some* calculated risk in there, we'll just get what everyone else gets. Investment managers too often just want to match other investment managers because it's seen as 'safe'. But that's not safe to me. Safe is using my skills and knowledge to work out how I can get the best outcome, especially in difficult situations.

There are very few people who truly earn the title 'leader'. Be one of them.

> There are very few people who truly
> earn the title 'leader'. Be one of them.

HELP OTHERS BUILD THEIR KNOWLEDGE

You know them – the ones who keep secrets, the ones who don't want you to know everything, withholding just enough to protect their position, their power, making you feel you're not quite as good as them, and definitely not at 'their level'. They're also the ones who don't realise they are limiting themselves, and at the same time, the respect they could be generating.

We don't own knowledge passed on to us. We are custodians. Knowledge is not only built from data, information and research. It's built from experience too. Help others build their knowledge through your experience. Pass it on selflessly, and while you're at it, see the respect held for you skyrocket.

Set an example

'You're the godfather.'

'What was that?' he responded, with incredulity.

'That's how you're seen,' the young employee said to this man.

He was taken aback – he had no idea. He was perplexed. He hoped of course she wasn't referring to a mafia-type godfather!

He knew there were others who were technically better than him. His strength however was how he got messages across, and he *did that by just being him.*

The most effective leaders are also trainers by default. The most powerful trait of a good trainer? Example setting. Just set an example. It is the number one ingredient.

KEY MESSAGE

You don't have to be an expert on everything. Be the one others aspire to be like; to emulate. They will mirror you; how you conduct yourself, your values, how you approach your work, how you care about your family, how you relate to others and look after them.

To set that example, they have to see us. We have to be with them, no matter what it takes.

CHAPTER 5

THE CONTRACTOR SYNDROME

It may seem odd, but so often pilots, and cabin crew as well, don't feel as much a part of an airline as you might expect, yet (and especially cabin crew) they are the 'face' of the company, along with ground staff.

These groups of employees are essentially remote workers in the sense that they don't work in an office with the rest of the wonderful people who make an airline run.

It takes an enormous effort to keep an airline functioning, and most of it is behind the scenes. The operational, safety, engineering and legal requirements are extraordinary. It truly is amazing how well they operate. There are so many factors that seem to transpire to get in the way of aircraft operating on time. This business is out there in nature, day and night, impacted by weather, air traffic, engineering, people, cargo ... it's endless. The profit margins are really quite small and the capital investment immense.

Our crews, particularly internationally but domestically as well, can go for ages without seeing staff members other than those they fly with. Whereas once there were many ground staff at airports supporting the operation (load control, crewing staff, flight planning and others), now, with advances in technology, most functions are electronic and can be accessed on an iPad. Conduct a flight overseas, and we can meet our crew and plan the flight without even going to an office. Fly home, and go home, literally.

Sometimes they feel excluded. In truth, they want to be a part of the company. They want to belong. They don't *want* to be excluded. Far from it. They don't want others to think of them as being privileged. They don't want to experience the tall poppy syndrome if it's evident in an organisation's culture (unfortunately, sometimes it is, even at this level). They just want to be a part of things, and respected, like anyone else.

You just can't engage with staff like that in a normal manner such as occurs in an office, where being together produces natural camaraderie.

KEY MESSAGE

You have to be out there with them. Yes, emails, newsletters and notices all have to be done, but there is no substitute for your physical presence. If you want to engage *everybody* in your organisation, and if you want to really know what's going on, you just have to be out there. That's leadership.

ENGAGEMENT

Let's talk engagement then . . .

So you like formulas? Here's one that works.

$$E = 3EI + 2D$$

How often do we hear about this thing called 'staff engagement'? All the time. Executives measure it, graph it, chart it, send us newsletters about it (sometimes playing with the figures and words to make it look like there's been an improvement), but in truth, too often they're missing the point.

Let me help.

For a start, there's nothing wrong with producing charts after an engagement survey but an improvement of 1%, 2% or 4% isn't reality. That's just a swing in the mood from time to time. It depends on the time of year, what's happened in people's lives, recent recruitment, the questions you ask – countless factors.

Please also, don't paper over bad news with words like, 'areas where we can do better'. Seriously. That just annoys the staff and makes things worse. It makes them even more cynical. You'll lose them for good. Say, 'areas where we're not doing well', or, 'have done badly'. Just use the words.

Now I know you like numbers. You're a businessperson, right? Maybe, but maybe you're not. Maybe you're an operational manager but your boss is in business. The executives certainly are.

This is business. Let's talk formulas for a moment then.

Let's convert this thing called 'engagement' and create something that maybe our business (note I said 'our' business) can use. Please do tell the HR Department about this because it falls squarely in their area as well.

Now this formula adheres to technical mathematical rules but the ingredients are derived from definitions and psychological reasoning – or personal opinion based on experience – which is where departure from mathematical convention occurs. Is it subjective you ask? Of course, and thank goodness. It's from me. (Thank you Dr Steve Holding for technical confirmation.)

Here it is:

$E = 3EI + 2D$

Where:

E = Engagement

EI = Emotional Intelligence

D = Decency

*Acceptability = acceptability of the manager by the staff (there has to be some level of **acceptability** or we will never engage). The question is, 'How acceptable?' The answer is, 'At least some. It doesn't have to be complete.'*

Acceptability = EI + Respect

Respect = EI + Decency

Engagement = Respect + Acceptability

    = (EI + Decency) + (EI + Respect)

    = (EI + Decency) + (EI + ((EI + Decency)))

    = (EI + Decency) + (2EI + Decency)

    = 3EI + 2Decency

    E = 3EI + 2D

Engagement = 3 parts Emotional Intelligence plus 2 parts Decency.

Engagement means having respect and acceptability.

KEY MESSAGES

- A demonstrable technical knowledge requirement for leaders is a given of course. They don't have to be the best but must be good at what they do and know. However, human beings need human contact. To appoint on a technical basis alone is akin to waving the train off at the station on the wrong track – wait for the inevitable engagement train wreck.
- What we want from all of this is a result. That's the whole idea. That's why we're going to all this trouble. It's *their* opinion you want, not ours. What they, the staff, want is what matters.

So then, how do you find out what they want?

CHAPTER 6

LESSEN YOUR CHANCES OF GETTING IT WRONG

ASK, DON'T TELL

Ask, ask, ask.

Source information.

Think.

Then make your decision.

The years are the '90s. Then, passengers could visit the flight deck, and sometimes remain for the take-off and landing. The flight deck door could remain open during the flight if we wanted. The cabin crew could enter the flight deck more easily. As we all know, that all changed following the World Trade Center attacks.

'The difference between you and us is we have time to sit and think. You don't.' Two of my doctor friends said the same thing on separate occasions when they travelled in the flight deck with me.

'If we have something to work out, we can review it, look it up, take time. You can't.'

Well, that's largely true. We are in constant motion, with fuel reducing. We are time limited ultimately. My friends were smart, and recognised it immediately.

It doesn't alter the fact though that to rush a decision can be disastrous. The first thing to do is to stop and do nothing. There are an infinite number of variables and associated risks. We don't want to add to them. We don't want to get it wrong. Only rarely is there a need to act immediately. It exists of course, but for the most part, no.

The first thing to do is to stop and do nothing.

We don't want to go down rabbit holes, box at shadows or follow red herrings.

With training and practice, we can all deliberately and methodically take the time to get it right, and act, even if time is not limitless. To do that, we need to use all our resources, and there are none better than your fellow workers.

KEY MESSAGE

Ask them. You will get the information you need, and it will also work wonders for the respect they hold for you.

But sometimes we end up with no other 'out'.

EXPECT THE UNEXPECTED. IT ALWAYS HAPPENS.

No more options

Darwin – Alice Springs – Adelaide – Melbourne.

It was a normal, and very enjoyable, flight pattern in those days. We'd first fly the opposite path, have 24 hours off and spend the night in Darwin, and return. It was a big day each way, but we had wonderful crew and that made it a very pleasant few days. There were nine of us. The Captain and First Officer, a Flight Engineer (on this Boeing 727), and six Flight Attendants.

Darwin overnights were always great. We'd relax, meet other crews who had flown in from other cities, and catch up for the evening. The return flight south departed just after lunch.

On this occasion, the weather for our return looked good at all cities except for Adelaide. There, it was anything but. Dust storms were forecast, reducing the visibility markedly. We'd be carrying as much fuel as we could.

We departed Alice Springs for Adelaide. It was an older aircraft. It didn't have the capability to carry as much fuel as today's aircraft. It might seem odd, but generally, aircraft can take off at a higher weight than they can land, even today. This means they have to reduce their weight through burning fuel before they can land, except for emergency situations. This is often a restricting factor when it comes to how much fuel can be loaded. More fuel can be carried on a longer flight. That's okay. The crews are good at working these things out and managing flights with these restrictions. So it was on this occasion – limited fuel.

Pilots each have defined roles and duties. The Captain is always the Captain, and the First Officer (FO) always the First Officer. In concert though, these are multi-crew aircraft. It takes two (and sometimes three) to operate them. One pilot will act as the Pilot Flying, and the other the Support Pilot (there are other titles, such as Pilot Monitoring). The duties for each are specified. It's very common for pilots to swap roles each flight. On this particular day, the First Officer was acting as Pilot Flying. Remember though that no matter what, the Captain remained in charge ultimately. First Officers operate as such also to gain experience for when they take up a Captain's role. This particular FO, Peter, was soon to take up a Captain position. He was very experienced and especially skilled at flying this aircraft.

There are policies that individual airlines adopt that specify circumstances under which each pilot shall revert to their Captain and FO roles, usually related to weather conditions or abnormal circumstances. Commonly a policy will be that, in poor weather, the Captain will fly the aircraft. In my view, there are circumstances under which it possibly should not always be the default position. I remember my Training Captain, the one who conducted my own command training, passing on his experience: 'Being in command is like being in command of a ship.' So true – sourcing information, making decisions, directing operations. There are times when there is no option, but in my experience, also other times when that's better achieved with the Captain in the support role, especially when flying with an exceptionally skilled First Officer.

We had decided we could carry sufficient fuel to fly from Alice Springs to Adelaide, make one attempt to land at Adelaide, and, if unsuccessful due to the weather, we could proceed to land at Melbourne. We would arrive at Melbourne with the minimum allowable fuel on board.

The world was quite a bit more free in those days. Security existed of course, but not to the extent that was to come following the events of September 11. So it was in the airline industry. Passengers were regularly visiting the flight decks for instance, including sometimes some very important people – like the leader of the National Party, Mr Tim Fischer, soon to become Deputy Prime Minister, who was on this flight. I knew he was on board. It's normal protocol for the Captain to be advised of any particular circumstances, people, cargo or any other requirements on the aircraft.

The Cabin Manager said, 'Chris, Tim Fischer has asked to visit the flight deck.' Of course, he – one of the politicians most respected across the political spectrum – was most welcome.

He asked of the weather. I said to him honestly that it was variable but not too good. He said he had a meeting to attend in Adelaide. He was clearly hoping to make it but of course was not pressuring at all. As a matter of professionalism, it wouldn't be a guiding factor in any case if anyone was. Safety is always number one. Nevertheless, we have a responsibility of course to deliver our passengers to their destination if possible, commensurate with safety. That's what we're paid to do.

Regular weather updates revealed the changeable weather continuing. There was a very large dust storm approaching from the north. This was South Australia. It had happened before. There was a 'front', a band of air moving across the state, powering the massive amount of dust – topsoil it had stolen from the landscape, from the desert, from the unbelievably huge properties that mapped the state like a giant jigsaw puzzle. Fronts can create a lot of turbulence. They slide quickly from ground level upwards, like a shovel, angled backwards. As it does, it scoops up air in front of it, pushing it upwards.

Wherever possible, aircraft land 'into the wind', which reduces speed over the ground and the length of runway required to land (and to take off).

This night, with a northerly wind, we were landing into the northeast.

We descended. The weather front was approaching Adelaide. There was a wall of dust and sand. We positioned ourselves to the west of the airport readying for the approach. Unfortunately this particular approach – landing to the north – did not allow a descent to as low a minimum altitude as the other end, landing into the south.

These aircraft fly fast. We were reducing speed progressively. To fly slowly, we have to make the wings larger by extending the sections at the back and front of the wings, the 'flaps' and 'slats'. Those wing sections can only be extended at slow speeds otherwise they will be overstressed.

We were west of the airport heading south, abeam the airport flying a left-curving flight path leading to the straight final approach, when, suddenly, we found out exactly where the front was. Right *here*. Flying through the angled air mass, the speed changed instantly. The momentum of this heavy aircraft resisted the change. Speed increased markedly, by around 30 knots. This immediately exceeded the flap extension maximum speed. As strong as they are, the flaps could be damaged. As a result, they needed an engineering inspection, and right then, that was a problem. This aircraft was now restricted. Not only are there maximum speeds to consider, but the flaps are not permitted to be extended above 20,000 feet, and the flaps on our aircraft can't now be retracted. We normally cruise at 35,000 feet or so. Does it matter? Absolutely. We fly high because we burn much less fuel at higher altitudes, and fly faster. Our fuel remaining would not be enough for flight to Melbourne. The option has gone. Just like that. We have to get into Adelaide.

We were busy, focused, but had come to terms with our new circumstances. The flight deck had three crew, concentrating heavily. As we progressed, some discussion – as if it was necessary. But it was. We needed to ensure everyone was clear. Okay, well we had the fuel we would have had available for Melbourne to use trying to land at Adelaide. How much do we have then? How much time? Figures and numbers were verbalised. The difference between what pilots do and many other professions is that they can't stop and think endlessly. The situation is fluid. It is time limited by fuel – potential energy reducing constantly.

Flying is like that. What a brilliant system global aviation has developed – probability and risk, proving it can be magnificently managed. The variables are countless.

> ## What a brilliant system global aviation has developed – probability and risk, proving it can be magnificently managed.

We followed the defined plan and flew on to final approach. We still had no visual reference.

Unexpected event number 2.

There was another aircraft, a light twin-engine eight-seat aircraft, ahead of us, but they fly slower and ATC, as talented as they are, and they are, are not mind readers. The aircraft ahead was flying even slower than they had anticipated. We were too close behind them, and closing. ATC issued an instruction to us to 'go around'. It's a manoeuvre to discontinue an approach, climb, follow a certain flight path and climb up to a safe altitude. It can be initiated by, as in this case, ATC, or by pilots at any stage, should they deem it the right course of action. It often comes as a surprise to passengers and can be disconcerting for first timers because of the dramatic change from a settled, generally steady approach to the application of lots of engine power. The aircraft rapidly climbs. In reality, it could be thought of as just a return to a take-off again, but from an airborne position.

We conducted the manoeuvre, with me concealing my annoyance for the moment. We did not have the luxury of wasting an attempt to become visual and land. I felt sorry for the Air Traffic Controller, who was working hard in horrendous conditions. He had, by this time, become aware of our situation. My next radio call to ATC expressed our position, assertively. In short, 'Please keep us away from anyone else.'

'Just put it on the ground'

We restarted the approach again, west of the airport. The weather front was there before. It was still there, a little further south. We flew through it again. It was rough. The dust storm had well and truly engulfed the airport, and Adelaide.

Final approach. 'Clear to land,' said the controller.

The turbulence was very strong. It was not easy to read the instruments. The aircraft was shaking. This was a very stable aircraft however, magnificent to fly, and virtually everyone's favourite at the time.

We looked from instruments to outside, instruments to outside, waiting for the runway to come into view through the horrendous dust. The visibility had been down to 100 metres at times, way less than required to see the runway and land (think over two kilometres in this case). We were approaching the minimum altitude. Looking. Wanting. Needing. In a serious emergency, the authority existed to descend lower than prescribed, but that required equally serious justification.

They appeared, the 'approach' lights (lights indicating the runway was just ahead), just, eerily through the swirling dust. It was surreal.

Focus.

Follow your training.

Scan the instruments. Watch speed, rate of descent. Make the support calls.

The FO was doing a top-class job. We arrived above the runway. The wind was so strong. The aircraft was being buffeted. It was almost impossible to read the instruments. We were just above the runway. The engines were back to idle and we were waiting for the aircraft to settle and touch down. It didn't happen when we expected it. The wind was maintaining our airspeed when we wanted it to reduce. The wings were developing more lift than we wanted.

One sentence from me: 'Just put it on the ground.'

The First Officer responded immediately by moving the control column definitively forward. We landed, nice and firmly, just as we wanted.

Taxiing clear of the runway, very slowly, we completed our after-landing procedures.

The aircraft was grounded for an engineering inspection.

As a crew, we talked about the whole event; how it unfolded, how we handled it, how quickly things change.

Flight complete.

Welcome to Command, Peter.

Expect the unexpected. Deal with it. You don't have a choice. You'll make your meeting, Mr Fischer.

> Expect the unexpected. Deal with it.
> You don't have a choice.

KEY MESSAGE

It will come, and when we least expect it. We'll be painted into a corner and we won't like it. We can't hide; can't pretend it's not happening. All eyes will be on us.

Whether it's a newborn needing to be looked after by a parent, a child needing to feel safe at school, an employee needing a sense of wellbeing at work, or the community wanting our governments to look after us and keep our families safe and secure (and we get pretty upset when we don't think they are), everyone wants to be looked after. We all have to step up sometime.

Others are relying on you. Use your command authority if you have to. Do what you have to do. Be proud that you did.

We are being watched all the time, every day. The way we treat our staff will come back to us . . . hopefully not like this next example.

CHAPTER 7

IF WE TREAT THEM POORLY, WE REAP THE CONSEQUENCES

'YOU CAN'T GO AROUND DOING THINGS LIKE THAT'

'You'll never guess what happened,' the Captain, Steve, said to me, then a young First Officer. It had been a long day.

'I was called into the office. The manager asked if I'd given away a bottle of wine to a passenger.' A staff member had reported him.

'"Yes," I said, and I relayed the circumstances that led to it.' They seemed reasonable to me.

'I was reprimanded. "You can't go around doing things like that," I was told. But I used my judgement. And besides, one movement of the thrust levers and we'll burn the equivalent of a *dozen* bottles of wine.'

He was right.

It's uncomfortably common, unfortunately, for a staff member to be reprimanded if they've been reported by another staff member, rather than have their manager stand up and support them. He was

52

clearly totally disgusted by this. It had been playing on his mind, and we were on the last flight of a tiring shift.

'Let's hold a competition. You're going to run it,' he said.

What did I have to do?

'Let's get the passengers to guess the outside air temperature and write it on their boarding passes to give to us. To give them a fair chance, we'll tell them it's between minus 40 and minus 50 degrees Celsius, but they have to guess it to the nearest tenth of a degree. Winners get a bottle of wine.'

Almost the whole aircraft played the game.

'But Steve, what do we do if there's more than one right answer given to us?'

This man was clearly very experienced. 'That never happens,' he said.

'How's that?' I asked.

'Because we're the only ones who really know the answers.'

We gave away three bottles of wine.

KEY MESSAGE

There's nothing like experience. Oh yes, and do respect your staff. Treat them well and stand up for them if need be.

As we mature in our leadership positions, we need to take the time to step back and think for ourselves. What do we *really* think about things, not what others think? Let's now think about *that* for a minute . . .

CHAPTER 8

BE WARY OF MANTRAS – HERE ARE JUST A COUPLE . . .

'NEVER GIVE UP, NEVER GIVE UP, NEVER GIVE UP, NEVER . . .'
So often I hear this said, especially in leadership circles. It worries me, a lot. People do have a strong tendency to latch onto mantras and live their lives according to them, without even questioning the basis for them. Remember, they were started by someone, just another person, sometime back in history, based on *their* own experiences or beliefs. That's *all*. We usually have no idea who that person might have been or anything about them.

Now, I'm very happy to declare that my own parents also told us to never give up, and I have immense respect for them. Their intent was always good. As someone who has worked in the mental health field however, and more importantly, as a parent, I've added something to it . . . and that something? 'Never give up . . . *until you've done your best.*'

Without that addition, it's potentially dangerous. We're not at war here. If we're talking about daily life, we need to be careful. There are some things that we just won't achieve, no matter what, and that's okay. No-one should feel any less of themselves if they can't, if they've done their very best. To expect more than a person's best is simply unfair.

By 'give up', are we talking about 'stopping'? The connotations of these can be both different and the same. It's how we perceive it, or *want* to perceive it.

Surely we're not talking about 'giving up' in the sense that we're throwing in the towel when we have more to give. It's about *stopping*. If we're talking about stopping, it's about being satisfied that we've given our best, and we know it. We'll know it when we look at ourselves in the mirror and speak to ourselves honestly.

> If we're talking about stopping,
> it's about being satisfied that we've
> given our best, and we know it.

At a weekly management meeting, I heard the firm's accountant, upon hearing of a staff member who made a mistake, make the statement, 'Once', with a smart look on his face, without so much as an assessment of why the error occurred. He was overtly playing – *playing* – the strongman role around the boardroom table. I might add that this was the very same person who closed his office door in a hurry, when he himself held a meeting at which an attendee made a statement that made him frightened that the Managing Director, in the office next door, may have overheard. It's cowardly behaviour.

Your staff can only do their best. We cannot expect any more. We cannot penalise them if they've done their best.

'Stopping' – accepting that we can't achieve something – does not diminish a person. It does not reduce authority. Are we a failure if we can't do something? If someone has honestly done their best, they should not have to 'prove' anything else, including even living up to a parent's expectation.

I know of one case when a mother said to her successful adult son, in front of her friends, 'You almost made it, didn't you?', with a smile on her face. Her friends were horrified. He had achieved wonderfully in his professional and personal life. In truth, this was about her feelings of inadequacy; her knowing deep down that she could have done better herself. It was about her desire for status. Her smile in truth was one of regret – that she had not fulfilled her own potential. The son would never have been able to please her.

The worst thing? He was barely even affected by her demeaning statement, such was his exposure to it and his blind loyalty, love and admiration for his mother.

Later, much later, he began to think, and to reject. He was the kind, polite one in the family. He didn't lose those traits, but he didn't accept this treatment any more either. Had it been someone else, it could well have been mentally disastrous.

KEY MESSAGE

Never stop . . . until you've done your best.

'A LEOPARD DOESN'T CHANGE ITS SPOTS'

This is just too big a statement. Yes, there are cases I'm aware of that this is certainly correct (as can be in certain cases of criminality as I understand it) but to accept that this applies across the board I think is simply wrong. I have seen incredible turnarounds and changes in people, in their relationships and professional lives, and permanent ones. If we were to live our lives by this tune, we may as well give up on people. I won't do that. I have too much proof to counter it.

> I have seen incredible turnarounds and changes in people, in their relationships and professional lives, and permanent ones.

When it comes to relationships, some even use this mantra as a weapon against others, not giving them an opportunity to change. Those people though usually have an agenda. They want to win something. Our attitudes are set at a very early stage in life and only another major event can change them.

I had a colleague who repeated this mantra over and over. In reality, she was a very jealous person, extremely judgemental, and was one of the best protagonists of tall poppy syndrome I've ever witnessed, using it to cut others down. The result was that she was diminishing herself in the eyes of those around her. It was sad to watch and listen to.

KEY MESSAGE

It is possible for a leopard can change its spots. It just has to want to.

Sure, listen to others, but it's okay, and right, to question. Your own judgement is just as valuable and worth listening to as anyone else's. It's dangerous to accept mantras blindly. Some are fine but a good dose of scepticism is healthy.

The sad cases are those where a person has lived by a certain mantra, only to think again late in life and wish they had not done so.

You can create your own mantras. You can change the world too. And yourself.

I don't want my legacy, what I pass on to others, to be just repetition of someone else's thoughts. I'll hear what others have to say, take what I think is right, question if I need to dig deeper, and add to it, like this . . .

CHAPTER 9

PROVIDE A LICENCE TO LEARN

'THE FAILURE RATE GOES UP'

It's the biggest single step in a pilot's career, promotion from First Officer to Captain – as it should be. From then on, it's all in your hands. The aircraft, the crew, the passengers, the company's reputation – and the rest.

Typically, it takes 10 years or so for the opportunity to arise, but that can vary markedly depending on so many local and global factors that affect a company's growth – the economy, retirement waves, travel trends, to name a few.

So often I've heard it (and thought it myself) from younger, less experienced (and more humble) pilots – words along these lines: 'I'm just happy I didn't have to make that decision today'. Be it a diversion to another airport, the amount of fuel to be carried, a report to be submitted, a non-standard decision (justified at the Captain's discretion), a disruptive passenger offload, continuation beyond a point of no return, making an approach (or not) to an airport in marginal weather, a decision to not depart (affecting the travel plans of hundreds) – countless events occur every day. They will. There are so many moving parts, all potentially transpiring to interrupt flights – engineering requirements, weather, crew availability, passengers, disruptions, air traffic. It's endless. Frankly, it's amazing airlines keep their schedules as well as they do, although it may not seem that way to the public. Most of all though, pilots are out there in nature. No two flights are exactly the same. Conditions change all the time. Pilots just have to deal with it.

It's one thing to be second in charge, but quite another to be where the buck actually stops. Those really big decisions, the ones with real ramifications, take some time to reduce in intensity, but they do, over time, and there's only one way to have them truly shrink. Experience. Which becomes leadership.

> It's one thing to be second in charge, but quite another to be where the buck actually stops.

Whether you're succeeding in attaining a command position or taking up a management role, it's just the start. Now the real learning begins. We all get it wrong sometimes – that's guaranteed. Often our operational or technical skills decline a little as our focus changes from operational matters to sourcing information, negotiating and making decisions. That's normal too. Most of all though, we learn about ourselves, our strengths and, more importantly, our weaknesses. If we don't, we're going to stagnate. We don't want to be the same leader at 50 that we were at 35. If we are, we haven't developed, haven't learned, haven't been honest with ourselves.

The really smart leaders also realise they have to take a step back when they take on a new position. Do nothing initially. That's what happens first in the flight deck when an emergency arises. Nothing. That way we reduce our chances of making a critical mistake. Think, then act. And when we're really taking on a totally different task (like writing a book), know that we're not 'in command' any more. We have to learn, again.

A memorable statement I heard many years ago, from an experienced person whose job was to plan training, was: 'When a new Check Captain is appointed, the failure rate goes up.'[1] How true. There are new programs in place now to reduce that rate, but the principle remains. A new examiner still hasn't had the priceless exposure needed to really know what the standard is out there. We initially may think so, but no, not really. It can be disconcerting to say the least to be checked by a person new to the role, or to work under a new manager.

I might add that there are some, a few in any role, who just don't ever alter with experience, but they are few and far between.

WHAT ARE YOU REALLY SAYING?

I've heard a lot of statements from supposed leaders over the years. Here are just a few. Be careful. Let's consider what they really mean.

- 'The standard is yours. That's why you were promoted.'
  Sure, but what is the overall standard, really? It takes some time to find that out, and when you're dealing with others, know that to try to take people up to a higher standard too fast or too high in one go will – more often than not – not work. In fact, it could have the opposite effect.

---

1   A Check Captain is a pilot who performs an oversight and safety role for pilots undergoing evaluation.

- *'The distance from the right-hand seat to the left is a lot more than one metre.'*
  So true. Taking up leadership roles is much more than just doing the same task with a new title.
- *'He missed by 300 feet. Where do you draw the line?'*
  We won't know until we find out if 300 feet is normal or not. Only then can we make a valid judgement. Maybe it's not the person, but the system.
- *'I've never been in this situation before. No-one's told us about this circumstance.'*
  Correct. It's not possible to pass on every single piece of knowledge or experience. Life is like that. Even when we're parenting, so much is a 'first'. Our children can't be expected to see it that way, but it's true. First house. First child. Second child is the first time you've had a 'second' child. First day at school. First time you've had another child at school. On it goes. We draw on our experience and knowledge and do our best as we go. When our children become adults, tell them this. It will open their eyes to really appreciate us.
- *'Your knowledge is excellent, but your wording is not as per the book.'*
  Does it matter, really? Often yes – and often no. Think about it.
- *'We can't do it. It'll set a precedent.'*
  Yes, maybe a good one. Policies cannot be written to cover every single circumstance. So often the fallback position for a new manager is to a policy or system. The system is supposed to run the operation. It's true, and that's why we build systems, to manage overall operations at a macro level. People are not machines, however. There will always be a

need for the occasional intervention. Leaders will have to exercise judgement, to back that judgement, and to wear some criticism as well. That comes with the job.

- *'If you do this, you'll fail. If you do that, you'll fail.'*
  Maybe, but say it like that and you're setting the scene for poor performance. It's always in the 'how'.

- *'If I was an examiner, I would have failed you.'*
  I heard someone say this. Be careful what you say. It had better be right. The person being assessed will one day be in a leadership position and will know whether you were right or not. Oh, and the fellow *was* an examiner. Why then didn't he do it? Lack of conviction? Fear? Actions can be so telling of human nature.

KEY MESSAGES

- Listen. Look. Ask. Find out why things are as they are before changing anything. To not do so is to risk ending up right back where you started, and it can come at great cost – financially of course, but reputationally for sure.

- . . . and no matter what, don't become a wolf in sheep's clothing or a smiling assassin. Be real. Be genuine all the time. Don't have one persona when you're in the office and another outside.

Now, let's look way beyond the staff ID card for a while, and learn who is sitting in the very same office or at the end of the email address, and how phenomenal so many are.

PART II

JUST WHO ARE YOUR CREW, REALLY?

CHAPTER 10

THEY'RE NOT ONLY WHO YOU THINK THEY ARE . . . AND YOU *REALLY* NEED THEM

'You've got 30 days to fix it'

'Well, that couldn't have gone much worse,' said the Managing Director, the moment the Civil Aviation Safety Authority representatives left the premises.

'Chris, I know it's not your fault, but we have to fix this.'

Around the table on the balcony overlooking the airport were the heads of each of the major departments of this small company.

It was silent. The mood understandably sombre. We had been given an ultimatum.

In summary: 'You have 30 days to fix it or we shut you down.'

This was the upshot of the most critical of all meetings for this organisation, a company being rebuilt out of the ashes of a poorly regarded business.

We had 30 days.

There were 32 Requests for Corrective Action (RCAs). That was a lot. The year was 2002. These RCAs dated back to 1998. Unheard of. Unacceptable.

This was not doable.

There were around 120 employees at the time dependent on the success of this company, let alone the investments of the owners. A core group of six people formed the nucleus of the Flight Operations Department. We had four aircraft and two different aircraft types (two of each).

The manuals were a mess, with some irrelevant, out-of-date information and procedures, and in one particular chapter there were no pages. That's right, no *pages* in that section. Other chapters referenced helicopter operations. Helicopters. We didn't have any helicopters.

This was going to be a massive rebuild, not only of the fundamental technical side of the operation, but reputationally, and my reputation would either be built along with it or annihilated, along with my fellow managers. I knew that.

There were some other ingredients. It was an incredibly difficult place to work. The culture was dreadful. Staff had no regard for management; indeed, fear and detestation for the managers would be an understatement. I was to find out why over time. In short, this was 'normal' for this company. Managers knew no other way and the culture had long been embedded, perpetuated over decades. Was it the fault of current leadership? Certainly they have a responsibility for a *present* state, but we should consider that they know nothing else, no other way. Having said that, it was clear there was a mutual distrust between managers and staff.

Still, maybe I could do something about it.

I'd been with this company for not much longer than a month.

Lying awake in the small hours of the morning, I knew this company could no longer keep its head in the sand and kid itself that the problems would all go away. This was make or break. This company was on the verge of being closed down, and now. This time, things would have to be done properly. The alternative was to be literally out of business. Not only that, but our owners needed direction upwards as well. They were naive as to how the business should be functioning operationally. I realised I had to assume nothing.

There were some great staff already there, but a time warp had enveloped the company and with that, dated and often inefficient policies remained embedded. They were tough and fierce operators, but the problems in the operational area were not their fault.

The potential however was huge, and true to my own beliefs and values, from a low base we could make great change.

The first thing? Keep it alive. Recognise when you're not in a strong position. We were in the weakest.

Next? Gain the trust of those you need – in this case, CASA, my managers and staff.

Triage my managers and CASA immediately so we remain in business and can at least pay some wages.

What did I do? I did what is commonly regarded as the antithesis of what management would normally do – openly invited the regulator in. Involved them. Not hiding. Gained their trust in what we're doing. This was crucial, and ultimately successful. It allowed us to remain operating while we addressed the problems. It would have been easier to shut down, fix the failures and restart, but that was fraught. A recommencement was never guaranteed, at least not to a fixed timeline, and there were livelihoods to consider. And I was confident we could mitigate operational risk, so long as we retained daily control. But that wasn't easy. Extreme commercial pressure, a difficult operating environment, highly limited resources and low morale are not a good mix.

In any case, I had chosen this path, be it different, and that was that.

My staff, those wonderful people who worked for and with me, I will never be able to thank enough. 10- and 12-hour days. Unbelievable pressure. Writing. Deciding. Doing. Meeting. Negotiating. Never stopping. Pressure on their home life.

I was leading them but they were the experts in their respective fields, not me. Under normal operating conditions, normal hierarchy reigns. Under 'emergency circumstances', the specialists, those with the knowledge and skills, reign supreme.

Our situation was critical; an emergency by any measure.

I let them run; trusted them.

If we want to degrade our staff's performance, micromanaging is a great way to do it. So too is being overbearing or negative. Loosen the reigns. Let them run. Let them perform.

Far from diminishing my authority, it enhanced it immeasurably. That's what 'command' is – earning authority such that it never, or rarely, has to be called upon.

> ## That's what 'command' is – earning authority such that it never, or rarely, has to be called upon.

In very basic terms, think of a professional boxer, being taunted by others who don't know of his or her skillset, and the boxer not using their 'power' because they don't have or want to. They know full well that they could defeat the aggressor, but no. Perhaps on occasion a small hint may be necessary as to what sits behind the calmness, but ever so rarely.

KEY MESSAGES

- Humility is power. In fact, it's better than power. It's influence, permanently.
- Without your staff, there is no CEO. You need them.
- Trust them. You have to. They will make mistakes. So will you. Make them. Learn. Move on.
- When the impossible is presented to you, accept where you are. Accept when you're not in a strong position. Talk. Listen. Find another way. You can. They're depending on you.
- Back yourself. Be different. Do 'different' if you have to.

Nine months later, those 32 RCAs were gone. The company did not close. It went on to become the darling of the aviation industry, and to grow massively.

My managers? Unsung heroes. Thank you to all of them.

We just don't know who's walking down the street beside us; what their lives are really like. Let's now meet some of your staff. I meet types of people like these a lot, and more commonly than you might think. Each has their genesis in the endless different backgrounds we

have, but also the many experiences we have, and how they affect us.[2]

In the following chapters we are going to explore some of the issues your 'crew' may be dealing with, which you may not even be aware of. It's important for you as a leader to understand what problems your people may be facing. Please be aware that in among the uplifting, there are some confronting issues we face in these chapters.

---

2   The attributes of the characters in the following chapters are real. Any similarity
    to anyone specific is purely coincidental. And all of these issues apply to both
    women and men. I've chosen male and female characters according to my
    firsthand experience of where I most commonly see these issues.

CHAPTER 11

JULIET: OUR UNHEARD WOMAN

Six hours into the flight, darkness has come much more quickly by virtue of the direction of our flight – we're heading east, with the sun setting behind us.

Darkness can be a natural sleep enhancer, as many of our passengers discover. The later model aircraft windows can be colour-changed, to block out sunlight but also inducing a mood change.

The flight deck is dark too, the lights dimmed for night flight.

It's time for a change of crew in the flight deck, such are the lengths of many flights these days, and they're set to become longer still.

This is also the time, in the blackness of night, that I enjoy putting on a jumper, and, in disguise (as many pilots do) walking back through the passenger cabin, all the way to the rear galley to check on our cabin crew. What a pleasure it is to do that. They're wonderful people, looking after not only our passengers but the flight crew as well, and they do it as much as possible with grace and good humour. Sometimes not all passengers are easy to deal with.

Let's meet Juliet.

WILL SOMEONE PLEASE HEAR ME? PLEASE.
I'M EXHAUSTED.

There it is again, that look. I've seen it before. It's been there so often –
barely a fraction of a smile, lasting but a moment in response to any
comment, well meaning as it may be, her head bowed slightly, an air
of resignation.

Juliet – our unheard woman, her aura now becoming sadness
and loneliness – has almost given up. Surely someone understands.
Do they not get it? She's spent. No, not from work – she likes to work
hard. In fact, she likes her work. No-one understands what she's
feeling. That's the problem. It's not just hearing, or even listening.
It's . . . it's sensing.

There are so *many* unique Juliets (and 'Julius' equally). And, like
all of us, they may have intrinsic or undivulged matters, personal
ones, they're dealing with along with their occupational concerns as
well. *We just don't know what they're dealing with.*

I introduce just two, as they have appeared a lot recently.

This particular Juliet wants to dress beautifully. She wants to feel
and look this way. She wants to think beauty – for herself first, not
others. If they find her so, then that makes her happy too. What she
finds beautiful is not necessarily the same as others. She finds other
people beautiful, male and female – those with intellect, kindness,
compassion, decency, self-respect, self-belief, and with authenticity –
just genuine. This is Juliet's idea of beauty.

Not wanting to attract unwanted attention, she just wants to be
free to be herself, and happy.

She wants to be safe to do so. Absolutely Juliet, you should.

And she doesn't want to be gender stereotyped. Unquestionably
no, Juliet.

Still, these things play on her.

Meet another.

She knows the kind of person she wants – in her words, 'The partner every girl dreams about.' Of course it may not be *every* girl, but lots. This person is not the cool, movie star type, or the gym-built muscular one, or anything like that. Again, in her words, 'much, much more of a person than those.' She wants someone who overtly expresses love for her, and shows it. Someone she can respect, who respects her and who she can admire. She wants someone she can look after, who is devoted to her. This Juliet loves the idea of having the car door opened for her, not because she needs it, but because they just want to do nice things for her. That's it.

She wants someone she can *truly talk to*, and who is genuinely interested in her day. Someone with depth.

'It's not asking too much, is it?' No Juliet. It's not.

'Maybe I have the problem.' No Juliet. You don't.

Juliet is of any age – she could be 15 or 95, and she *is* talking. People aren't listening. They aren't hearing. Oh, they genuinely believe they are, even some who seem to be more emotionally tuned in, who with the best of intent truly do focus on words and listen with care, but honestly, most still don't understand her. She doesn't feel heard because they're 'listening' for the wrong thing. It's the *visceral* she wants us to hear – 'hear' the feeling, the emotion, the instinct. She wants you to not only know, but to really *want* to know. Dig deeper. Can you imagine the level of frustration Juliet must be feeling? Not being able to literally *communicate*? That's exactly what it is for this Juliet. It's a fundamental human need. It's crushing her. She's lonely, and she's exhausted. She is a tormented soul.

Moreover, she doesn't want others to 'fix' things for her. Please, no. That will make it worse because it just proves we're not understanding her and she's going to feel obliged to try to explain herself even more. We're not hearing her frustration. If we're trying to fix it, we're actually insulting her.

That's what fixing others' problems does. It subliminally says to them they don't have the ability to fix their own problems.

At work, she feels like she has to justify herself more than others. It's not just because she's a woman but because she wants to be heard, and to do that, she feels her work must be more overt, more apparent, of a higher standard – just *better*. Unfortunately, some, often those with a shallow view of the world, like a veneer, take issue when she does this. They often feel threatened by it, and have a desire to hold her back. I know. They tell me. They have difficulty with it. There are reasons for their responses – inadequacy, insecurity, discomfort, confusion. But the problem is theirs. This is incredibly important.

KEY MESSAGE

If someone else is making us feel any of those things, or upset or angry, it tells us more about us than them. Maybe we've reached our own limit with them, people like them, or a particular issue. It doesn't mean we're wrong. The person may still be incredibly difficult, but maybe we should remove ourselves from the situation, or at work hand over to someone else. And it's probably time we sought help ourselves.

Then there are those who *do* understand but who aren't strong enough to break away from their own peers and support that person. The proportion of true leaders in the world, those who will overtly stand up for something or someone, is just so low.

> The proportion of true leaders in the world, those who will overtly stand up for something or someone, is just so low.

The cycle continues. She feels like she's not taken seriously. Compounding it, Juliet is often someone who doesn't like confrontation, so she accepts it; just accepts it. On the rare occasion she does reach her breaking point, if pushed, really pushed, she will react, strongly, and stand up for herself – and if she does, it takes people aback. 'This is not the Juliet we know. She must be suffering some personal problems. Give her some space, some time off. She'll settle down.'

Sure, back to the Juliet *we* can accept? I don't think so. No-one should feel a need to be a chameleon. We have no right to make someone else feel like this, to live their life like this. That's not freedom.

We don't have to lose ourselves. Ceasing being authentic catches up with us eventually. It's insidious, and dangerous.

I hear you, Juliet. I do. I also know you're everywhere, so tell me about you Juliet. I really want to know.

CHAPTER 12

OSCAR: OUR UNSPOKEN MAN

'Happy Tuesday!'

'Good morning, everyone.'

A chorus of replies across the office, 'Good morning, Oscar.'

'Happy Tuesday!', from a particularly exuberant young female administration staffer, clearly trying to make her way up the corporate ladder.

Lovely, intelligent young woman, Oscar says to himself. He thinks very highly of her. They had such a rapport and wonderful conversations. She would seek him out for 'one of our great talks' as she called them. He also thinks she's an incredible asset to the organisation, with talent yet unrecognised. Bright. Cheerful. Still young however and gaining experience, both professionally and personally. Oscar is a true father. Protective. He can't help but be so. By *his* standards (he just can't use the word 'generation'. It makes him feel old, and he doesn't want to feel so.), she is a little coquettish at times and he worries she'll be taken too literally or taken advantage of by potential suitors – or users. He's seen

78

it before. He doesn't want her to be hurt. He *does* want her to be free to be herself.

But Oscar has other things going on in his head as he walks across the office. *I really hate this 'happy every day of the week' thing that's going on. Truly, I find it false and meaningless. It just devalues Fridays. I just have to play this stupid game I suppose and pretend I'm enjoying it.* No, he's not an angry man. As he would say, he's just 'over it all'. This is Oscar's day . . . day after day after day.

It's important you meet Oscar because he is everywhere. You may know him quite well; very well in fact. Is it you?

Oscar is typically 40 to 60 years of age, plus or minus a few years, although that age range is becoming younger. He is the primary breadwinner of his still quite traditional family, with two or three children.

Oscar is not tired of *being* 'the engine' that keeps the family unit running and financially secure, but *by* it . . . and what man is going to own up to that? What man is going to say that to his partner or family? Almost none.

As an organisational counsellor working with everyone from CEOs to new hires, I can say that we're not all that different. Those further up the organisational chart are simply coming off a higher base. Our problems, however, do not. But mental health is very egalitarian. It does not discriminate.

Mental health is very egalitarian.
It does not discriminate.

79

Oscar concerns me, a lot.

Of course, there are lots of different kinds of family units and 'engines', but this is Oscar – and he really is everywhere. But it's not the family unit that's causing issues for Oscar. It's occupational and societal demands; expectations. If these weren't so great, he could attend to his family more; *attend to himself* more. The usual family issues would be more manageable.

He is an extremely loyal and dedicated family man; very proud of his family, and he would literally do anything for them. In truth though, in the deepest recesses of his mind only visited by himself, there are times he doesn't feel appreciated, even by them. He knows he's not perfect. He makes mistakes. He does his very best though.

Oscar talks to himself, every day. *I just wish my family would talk to me, ask me about me. They don't really know me outside of being Dad and a husband. I want them to ask me what I think about things, and ask me about my life. I was a boy once, a happy teenager knocking around with his mates. I'm just doing my best. I think I've done a pretty good job, haven't I?*

Oscar has typically been working in his career since he qualified in his profession in his early 20s. Was this the career he really wanted to pursue? We don't know. Was he pressured into it? We need to ask him. We know this though: he feels he simply must keep the money coming in to pay for the school fees, the rates, the power bills, holidays, and a car or two. If he doesn't do that, the ramifications for his family would be unbearable for him.

He's had enough of what he terms 'commercial pressure'. He doesn't want to hear any more about productivity and profits – he can't give any more; the cost of living going up or the cost of housing – he knows all about it; saving for retirement – he's doing everything he can; staff engagement programs – he's seen and heard it all and he finds it false. He just sees these as a mechanism to make him work even harder, or as pressure to conform.

'Our customers like us,' a smart, up-and-coming manager tells the staff at a corporate love in, 'but we want them to *love us.*' Oscar, internally: *what infantile, false rubbish. Don't they get it? We have to love the company first. It's like going to the supermarket and having the checkout person use some disingenuous rehearsed line, supposedly to put a smile on the customer's face, no doubt prescribed for them by some immature manager. Just let these people be their natural happy self.*

He's tired of status anxiety, feeling he should build a bigger house to be accepted in the neighbourhood. Our Oscar doesn't know about the technical term for it. He just experiences it. He's too close to it. He's in it. He can't see. He just can't see.

He's just trying to build what most men want and that's their very own 'sheep station'. For Oscar, that means his home, super-annuation, security and safety for his family, holidays; a good life for them all.

He's reached his limit with managers who he says 'don't get it' – they don't realise for instance that continually putting emails out with bold or underlined words to make a point insults him. (Yes, he and his fellow staff members talk about this a lot in the lunchroom.) To Oscar, there's always some threat, perceived or real. It doesn't matter. If he feels it, it's real to him.

Oscar doesn't really feel free – he doesn't know what that feels like. Let's also not mistake him for a quiet person, or an introverted person either.

He thinks, *I'm a non-human, a resource.*

And, *I've tried antidepressants. I was great while I was on them but when I stopped, the problems were still there. I want them fixed. Oh yes, and my wife said I was just too happy while I was on them. That made it even worse. 'Snap out of it,' she said. I can't win.*

We have a silent epidemic of Oscars. I see this – men of a similar age – all too often, experiencing what they shouldn't, and for so many of them this is just how life is. Some don't even know they've had a problem until it's upon them.

Why is this? Why is Oscar as he is?

There are lots of circumstances, but let me describe a common one.

So many men, like Oscar, are in a river – *in* the river, not floating on top. They don't know anything else. The river was there, flowing before them. They were born into it. The River Oscar is a river of expectation, almost preordained. Society has trained him, almost obliged him, to fit into the mould, with insufficient or no regard to what Oscar wants – what makes Oscar truly fulfilled. By the way, often it doesn't take much to swing the balance. Sometimes he might like to get out of the river for a while, or at least be above water. That's more than okay. If he does, he isn't going to run away from his responsibilities. He wants them. They are his family, remember? So it is that he plays his part. Sometimes, much, much later, he starts to think, and realises something just isn't right. By then though, a lot of damage has happened.

He's become resilient, but perhaps also just too tolerant.

Oscar's resilience grew over the years as he was exposed to life's pressures. Up and up it went, increasing his ability to cope. Along with it, he became more and more tolerant. Tolerance and resilience though are two different things. We can become tolerant in a good way and not in others – like tolerating bad behaviour or excess pressure at work. It's insidious.

KEY MESSAGES

- There is no magic solution, but in the meantime, we need to help the Oscars of the world, to support and protect them. It may be as simple as finding out how they're feeling. If they're feeling 2 out of 10 and something makes them 3 out of 10, we might be able to help them to do more of it. We need to find out what that is of course, and we find out by talking.
- We need to learn to take the pressure off others as well as ourselves. We simply cannot, *cannot* expect people's resilience to continue to build, especially by virtue of exposure to life or organisational pressures.

Oscar, like all of us, couldn't be expected to build up his resilience endlessly though.

Increased pressure, increased resilience, increased pressure, increased resilience, increased pressure, increased pressure, increased pressure . . . no more resilience. This was Oscar.

He was sitting at his maximum – his 'redline' – even though he didn't realise it. That is a real problem, when we don't recognise it ourselves. All it took was one more thing to deal with – one more impact. It came, it hit him – hard. He hung on as best he could, but he was sliding, gently at first like he was on an icy slope, until he could hang on no more.

The slope became a cliff, and off he fell, and it was a vertical descent.

On a scale of 1 to 10, where 10 is feeling on top of the world and 1 is suicidal, within a couple of days, he hit 2. All he had built up over his life vanished in an instant.

Oscar. Shattered. Devastated. A shell.

He could sit in one chair, in one place, looking in one direction only.

No darkness. No small rooms.

A 2. So dangerously close to 1.

It's hard to believe this is the same man.

To him, life had changed forever. It was like everything he knew had vanished; taken from him by someone else. He just could not understand any of it. He's been such a good person. He couldn't have given any more.

Oscar though is lucky. There are three others who become aware of what's going on for Oscar, and don't leave him alone for a minute. Too much can happen in a minute.

Over the course of a week, his descent into an abyss continues, slowed only by those three. In truth, they are still not fully aware of his state. He doesn't reveal all. He reaches 1, and stays there. It took about a week.

Then he realises. It hits him. He can make this stop. He lifts, instantly. He rises from 1 to 3. Relief. Some weight is lifted from his shoulders. He almost thinks he's happy. Oscar is in serious danger now, but he doesn't realise it yet. He will, much later.

How then will he do this? He thinks hard. The car. A hose. It will be painless. Where will I do this? I don't want to shatter others, but he knows he will. Do I want to leave a message? All the while, he feels 'better', or thinks he does.

He meets with two of his friends, separately. They have never seen him like this. They are shocked and frightened. This is a different person. He can't even remember how he arranged to meet them – no memory at all.

He finds himself calling his doctor for an urgent consultation. It is Friday – such a long time until his Monday appointment. He is watched over virtually 24 hours a day. He sleeps on the loungeroom floor.

Medication. Two weeks for an improvement, apparently. He waits. On the third day, he spikes up for about an hour. It's amazing, but doesn't last, and doesn't come back. It makes him remember, however, happier times.

He calls a psychologist – an early appointment. He's lucky to get in quickly.

He sits at 1.5 for weeks. An unspoken ritual happens with one friend who calls or sees him every single day, without fail. This person is one of the three in particular he credits with saving him.

Oscar gives his friend his daily score: 2 . . . 3 . . . 3.5 . . . 4 . . . 3.5 . . . 4 . . . 5.5 . . . 4.5 . . . 6.

Months and months of the same – these people never abandon him.

Four months in, and Oscar reaches 7.5. Then the second crash. In one day, he hits 1 again. The *cause* of the initial cliff has not been dealt with.

The pattern returns. The danger of the '1 to 3'. Relief.

This time, a rope over the beam, he thought. But he escapes.

His friends are still there. They know.

'I was really worried about you,' says one.

'You had every right to be,' he replies. She goes ashen.

85

'What stopped you?' she asks.

He thinks for a moment, and then turns back to look at her. 'Hope,' he says. 'The most minuscule amount of hope.' There was nothing else.

Ask Oscar if suicide is a choice, as is a common mantra, and you'll be met with a quick rebuke: 'Absolutely not. A person with a terminal illness who can't get access to voluntary assisted dying would be making a choice, not someone else, unless you're totally disregarding their state of mind.' People commonly say it's a choice; so often however that's a reason to excuse themselves from blame or having had any degree of impact. No matter our views however, if anyone deserves to be heard, it's Oscar.

Oscar these days? It's a sawtooth recovery. His suicidal thoughts are becoming fewer. Fewer, but they still occur.

There are other Oscars – like the one who goes out to the bush. He goes there to 'think'. He has stopped himself from taking his own life there numerous times. Let's hope he continues to do so.

WHAT CAN WE DO?

Take note of changes in a person's demeanour, or maybe the way they dress. Are they giving things away? Perhaps they're even feeling at peace all of a sudden. That's a potential alarm bell ringing right there – when someone feels a sense of relief at the prospect of a way to stop the pain.

There is a much bigger picture here though and we, as a society, must have a serious conversation, and we need to be brutally honest with ourselves, and courageous. What are we doing to create this crisis? It didn't just occur for no reason. We need to look at the total environment we're living and working in – everything, from our built environment to our nurse–patient ratios and everything in between – anything that creates increased stress, because it all does. There's too much inequality and unfairness; too much disparity. Conversely, there are those who just expect too much. We need leadership to get the balance right. This is a community we're supposed to be building, not a business.

There is a much bigger picture here though and we, as a society, must have a serious conversation, and we need to be brutally honest with ourselves, and courageous.

KEY MESSAGE

We simply cannot, cannot expect people's resilience to continue to build, especially by virtue of exposure to life's or organisational pressures.

There is a very lamentable and damaging bias towards punishment to control, rather than praise, and it's dreadfully contagious. It happens too often in workplaces, in society, and even in the home. Those who perpetrate it often use legal ramifications as justification for instituting another rule. Pretty soon, there's nowhere left to move without threat. People can't breathe. It's not a matter of being naive. We all know there are those who will do bad things, but we shouldn't make rules for everyone based on the behaviour of a small part of our community. If we keep that up, we'll actually create more problems, not less. Look at where we can reward the majority, rather than penalise to control a minority.

KEY MESSAGE

We know it takes more than talk to help Oscar, but that's the starting point. It's also important to know men however, and men generally want an answer, something fixed. We need to change our normal, collegial conversations at work and our friendship conversations to ones that scratch the surface just a little – not too much in case we scare the other person away, but just beneath the surface. 'Tell me about you.' To find out how Oscar is, we must ask him about himself. Only then will we find out how he's going.

Oscar, I know you're reading this. I know you are. I hear you.
'Good night, everyone.'
'Good night, Oscar. See you tomorrow.'

FREE TO BE HIMSELF

This Oscar is a 'visual' person. He likes to draw to describe. So it is that he drew his journey. This alone was cathartic, and it's Oscar 'talking' to us.

Two days was all it took, down to '2'. Importantly, Oscar was not at '10' (feeling great), at the top of his resilience curve. His 10 was about where he was happiest.

'Tell me when you were happiest, Oscar.' He says for him it's directly related to him being free to be himself, without so much external pressure or expectation. As the impact of external pressures reduced, his happiness increased. Others realised they had to take some pressure off him.

On the face of it, we might think that the more resilience Oscar developed, the happier he became, because he could cope better – not so. It didn't equate. Happiness has other ingredients.

Oscar became happier with each recovery because he felt listened to for the first time in his life. It took *his* crash though for others to look at themselves. They realised the impact they'd had on Oscar as well. They learned too.

KEY MESSAGE

We all need to learn to take the pressure off others as well as ourselves.

REPRISE

'Tell me about you.'

I see this – men of a similar age all too often experiencing what they shouldn't, and for so many of them, this is just how life is. Some don't even know they have a problem until it's upon them. And yes, of course women go through this as well, but I'm seeing this firsthand in men increasingly.

Asking others if they're okay is a good thing. The problem is though that we're missing a step. When we ask Oscar (again, Oscar is everywhere) that question, he will almost always answer, 'Yes.' He's not.

Say to them, 'Tell me about you,' and when they reply with, 'Why?', be ready to respond, '. . . because I really want to know'. They won't expect a question like this and may initially be wary.

Now here's the thing. This technique can be taught, and when learned, you, the questioner, are about to learn a whole lot about *you* too, and probably more than you'll learn about the person you've approached. Take note of your own reactions to what they tell you. Learn about yourself.

KEY MESSAGE

There is a step before we ask Oscar if he is okay. The trouble is, when we ask Oscar that question, he will almost always answer, 'Yes.' He's not.

I've learned this. Everyone wants to be looked after. A child wants to be looked after by a caring parent. A school student wants to be safe and looked after by their school, and yes, believe it or not, employees by their employers (no matter the industrial climate). Of course, business is business, but they're also communities of people, and people want to belong. So does Oscar, and he's not asking too much.

This needs to be normalised to become the way we do business. It's not hard. There's no downside and a huge upside.

CHAPTER 13

MICHAEL: HE JUST WANTED TO BELONG

A TIME FOR TRUTH

Many years ago, I was addressing a group of employees for an organisation at a time when the relationship between that group and management was at an all-time low. I knew that. I also knew that this was not the time for a veneer, a pep talk, which would have thrown fuel on the fire, driven engagement to oblivion and destroyed any semblance of respect I had left.

The air could be cut with a knife, such was the *depression* in that room. It was beyond tension.

This was a time for truth.

After some initial murmurings, one person stood up from his chair and said, 'We want to belong,' and with that, in they came, one after the other. 'Yes, that's it, because we don't.' The flood gates had opened. Release, finally.

Sometime afterwards, staff member Michael was awarded a significant promotion. He undertook training. Michael was bright, very bright, and his technical knowledge hard to fault. Upon successfully achieving his goal, he was provided with feedback which included a comment that, while his technical standard was exemplary, he needed to work on his interpersonal skills, especially for his future relationships with those who would be reporting to him. It was noted that, with the best of intentions, he was still too authoritarian. The gradient he set was just too steep.

This came as a real shock for Michael. He had no idea this was how he was perceived. This simply wasn't the Michael he had in his own mind.

Michael: 'I thought that's what you wanted to see.' To be a leader in his mind, there had to be a gradient – a steep one. That's how he thought he would gain respect. No Michael, we don't need our colleagues to call us by our title (if we have one), when in a closed, private workspace, away from the public eye, to gain respect.

KEY MESSAGE

In truth, with authoritarian behaviour, we'll get reluctant compliance at best, and probably only temporary conformity.

He was, as we all do, portraying an image. 'Image management' – displaying to others what he wanted them to see. Michael had been mentored poorly.

This feedback was just too much for him, however. Sure, he had some personal issues going on in the background. We have to be able to separate them from our professional life, completely. Really? Sure, most can do that to an acceptable level most of the time, but not always. Michael didn't come back to work for six months, and then only for a short time. He took his own life.

Michael became Oscar – just too many arrows to deal with.

Big lessons

Sometimes it can be too much for a person to be made aware of how they were perceived by others throughout their life. It needs to be done with great care.

There are big lessons here. We don't want to exacerbate an issue, let alone create one, even inadvertently, but this is happening every day, not just in our workplaces but in our private lives. We just don't have the level of emotional intelligence we should have, in or outside our workplaces; nothing like it, but it's not just a matter of educating leaders in the subject and expecting change. It doesn't work like that.

Sure, we may be running a business or organisation, but our business is a community of people, part of a society, and societies can't be run solely like a business. Societies run on a culture. We need cultural leaders too.

> Sure, we may be running a business or organisation, but our business is a community of people, part of a society, and societies can't be run solely like a business.

Be careful who you choose as a mentor.

CHAPTER 14

CYNTHIA: WEARING A MASK

'CYNTHIA, WHERE ARE YOU?'

She sits and looks at me, saying nothing, but in that silence, saying everything. She takes out her phone, places it on the table and presses play. It's a recording. Cynthia has now taken me to her kitchen. She's preparing a meal, or attempting to.

More on the recording later.

There are so many Cynthias. She is everywhere. Meet this particular Cynthia.

She is a professional person, earning a good income in a respected career. She has young children and always puts on a happy face, but it's a mask. How often I see this.

She asks to speak. She's having difficulties financially and personally and is needing support and assistance to obtain better work conditions. She says nothing more. The mask is firmly in place.

Of course, I'll try to help. We agree to speak again, but it's often difficult to catch up with her. One evening I succeed in reaching her on the phone but there's a lot of background noise.

I can hear a lot of vehicle and people noise, and her words are often unintelligible.

'Cynthia, where are you?' I ask. Quietness, then, 'I'm at work . . . ,' she replies; that, followed by an unconvincing laugh and a reluctance to speak. She's trying to downplay what she's about to reveal '. . . at my other job.' She's clearly self-conscious at revealing she holds another position. The mask is lowering, revealing more of her face; of her. I can 'see' her eyes more clearly now, however. There is a deep sadness in them; and resignation.

The background noise I hear is that of a busy school in a busy area. She does shift work as a school crossing controller. She's only half focusing on our conversation, doing the right thing – prioritising the pedestrians.

This is her second job. Turns out she has three. I don't ask what the third one is.

Evening work? Her chosen profession is not enough? Young children? Where are they? It would be reasonable to assume a partner is looking after them. Financial difficulties? Perhaps this family has fallen upon hard times. We just don't know.

It's in her voice, however. Something. There's more she's not saying.

Back to the kitchen.

The recording alone is enough – a tirade of abuse coming at her. Blaring, disgraceful ridicule. Belittling, demeaning, persecuting vilification. Chilling, frightening. I can hear the fear in her through the phone; her shaking voice; her acquiescence as she attempts to stay safe in the moment, to survive another night.

I can truly feel the weight of the air in that house that night – thick with threat.

The mask is down. The happy face is no more. You're exhausted, aren't you Cynthia. Frightened. Trapped. I know.

We can read about domestic violence, or see it on the news and feel shock, disgust and dismay. Yet here she is right in front of me, safe for now, revealing her private hell. When someone does that, exposes their vulnerability, you can taste it – the terror, the danger, the pain – and all this committed by a person who purports to love her and their children.

Revealed. It's all been false; a veneer, hinging on her ability to bring in money to support horrendous loans she's now responsible for, his anger no longer able to be contained as he blames her for his circumstances – he, unable to earn sufficient money to fund the lifestyle he aspires to (not so her, with simpler expectations) and he's at home, reluctantly looking after their children. Now she's living a nightmare.

What right does one human being have to do that to another – effectively destroying their life? None whatsoever.

I talk about the Cynthia, especially to groups of men (as well as women). I want to paint a picture for them. I want them to *sense* how it affects not just these women but a *man*, because it's men who can make the difference; make real change. Men should not be asking women to do this on their own. I don't want men to become desensitised to what they see on the news. It's real. It could be happening next door; any variation of our Cynthia. The victim could be someone close to you, now or in the future. It could be our daughters. Of course, domestic violence occurs both ways. Overwhelmingly though, the perpetrator is a man.

This is also about power over another, and it occurs in all sorts of ways. Fear. Control. Coercion. Physical. Verbal. Emotional. Financial. We cannot accept any of this. Our Cynthias should never have to.

WHAT CAN WE DO?

We see public condemnation of disrespect for women every day now. It's still not enough. If we're going to truly do something about it, we must think bigger, *much* bigger. We need cultural transformation. What sort of culture do we want to build for the future and how does it all weave together to look after Cynthia?

We have a big task, but we can do it. Of course, we need laws and policies, and we must enforce them vehemently, but we are also in serious need of role models to exhibit behaviour and conduct. We need to stem the human proclivity to feed our need for stronger words and actions to satiate our desires, like a more powerful drug, or stronger violence.

What can we all do though, each of us, and today, not tomorrow? Can we play a part, be part of the fix? Yes, we can. Let's not look at others, governments or law enforcement and expect them to do it all for us. It's our community. Where can we start? Well words are powerful, and free.

As yesterday's expletives and disrespectful expressions become today's seemingly valueless throwaway lines, we need the reappearance of role models of decency. We need to recognise desensitisation. It's not by any stretch to suggest we all become flawless – far from it – but simply to learn there should be a line, where the line is, when something really is beneath common decency, and when not to cross it, until it becomes intuitive. This usually doesn't

As yesterday's expletives and disrespectful expressions become today's seemingly valueless throwaway lines, we need the reappearance of role models of decency.

happen by itself. It takes a bit of maturing sometimes, and there are lots of children walking around in adult bodies.

There is, of course, the argument that all kinds of people use all kinds of language, but that doesn't provide an excuse or licence to not consider others any time we like. *This is supposed to be a community*. It's not all about self. Most of the time, I should add, people genuinely respect and warm to those who at least govern their language circumstantially. It's not hard.

Let's raise our children to expect that they have the right to not be demeaned, insulted or stereotyped, and to be streetwise enough to know that the rest of the world is not all there yet.

We can do this. Sense it, fellows.

KEY MESSAGE

Somewhere in your organisation, now or in the future, there will be a Cynthia. She may already be close to you. She is often superb at putting up a mask, but should never have to. Put yourself in her position – if you can, that is. It's often unimaginable. What would you want? Just leave? It's not always that simple.

We cannot let this go, ever.

CHAPTER 15

GABRIEL'S WAY: KICKING HIS ADDICTION HIS WAY

'YOU'VE GOT TO RELAX, MATE'

'No, I'll tell *you* what I've done,' he said to his GP. It's Gabriel – exhausted, exasperated, frustrated, frowning.

His doctor, 'Okay' – sitting back in his chair, slightly taken aback by this young patient, yet accepting him in his mature doctor-like manner, following which Gabriel, fluent, articulate, relayed everything he had tried to rid himself, and his life, of these unbearable headaches, now thieving his life daily.

'Well, you've done everything I would have told you to do.' The doctor looked at him with genuine concern. 'You've got to relax, mate.'

Gabriel was 24 years old, and he was addicted to codeine.

Two weeks later, one evening and with trepidation, he walked into an old 'hospital-like place', as he put it, located the room, and entered. There were some people already there, with others arriving.

It was immediately obvious no-one knew each other. They stood around awkwardly.

Chairs were set in a circle. A pleasant lady, with a warm, calm smile, welcomed them all, and invited them to take a seat. Gabriel had seen this sort of thing on television. He sensed what was coming. Never did he envisage he'd be living it. He's only 24, for goodness' sake.

They all learned about each other. *What is this?* Gabriel inwardly exclaims. *What am I doing here? How did I end up in this place?* The doctor had recommended relaxation therapy. *I'm surrounded by all these strange people. This is crazy. They're nutcases. This isn't happening.*

It then starts. Around the circle they go. People introduce themselves. State their problems. *Oh god – just like in the movies.* One Flew Over the Cuckoo's Nest. *I hate this.*

The therapist he estimates at about 40, although at his young age, he knows he really has very little idea. Everyone looks old. 'She's got that mature look, that's all,' he says to himself. Dressed in a calm, conservative outfit, she speaks in a quiet, kind voice, turning her head slowly around the room as each person speaks. *Person? Patient? What am I? I don't really know*, he thinks. She seems to be watching others simultaneously, as though to gauge reactions, or their understanding, to see perhaps if listening is helping them too. He sees how she even closes her mouth in a calm manner after she speaks; a slight nod of her head to complete a sentence. Her facial expression is one of genuine interest in each speaker, although she remains just a little removed. She is in quiet control.

He recalls some other people's issues. There is a lady struggling at home with a young baby – very stressed – and, oh yes, the young man, probably around 20 years old, continually applying to join the Army, but not passing the medical each time because his blood pressure would be too high. He becomes so anxious every time he tries to pass the medical that his blood pressure goes through the roof.

The session lasts for 90 minutes. There will be 10 of them – every Tuesday night. Gabriel wonders, *how will I get through it? . . . I can't tell anyone at work, especially in the aviation industry. They might ground me.*

And then the worst part of all. At 15 minutes to go, they are told to close their eyes. The therapist starts: 'Relax your toes. Relax your feet. Let them go. Feel them go limp.' The group is quiet. Gabriel wonders what everyone else is thinking. 'Relax your arms. Feel their weight resting on your legs.' He's trying to relax, but it's hard, just hard. It's not natural. This isn't him. Still, he does his best.

The therapist, almost solemnly, guides the group to unwind their entire body.

Then, quietness. Two minutes of quiet. Nothing.

With barely more than a whisper, she awakens their consciousness. They open their eyes. She has that look; the faint smile. They're finished for the evening.

We take a cassette, for our tape recorders. Yes, for Gabriel, this was some years ago. Yet it is only in recent years that he speaks of his experience.

They have homework to do: lie somewhere comfortable – the bed, the floor – in a supine position. It doesn't matter where. Close the eyes and listen to the relaxation recording provided by the therapist.

Torture. This is simply suffering for Gabriel. He tries, but his brain doesn't seem to switch off. Nevertheless, for 10 weeks, he does as he was asked, and at least tries.

The final night of the course arrives – a graduation of sorts . . . most hope. Gabriel has said little of his progress throughout, but has actually started to look forward to Tuesday nights, for the social aspect at least.

Around the circle the therapist goes, asking each how they are now that they have reached the end of the course. Of real note to Gabriel: the young mum is so much better. Her home is calmer, her baby more settled. She has a smile on her face.

That man had managed to pass his medical. Success! He's in the Army. The whole room is delighted.

'Gabriel, how are you? How did you go?' All eyes were on him, as they had been on each of their now 'course friends'.

'Well,' he started, 'I wasn't going to say anything until now . . . but . . . I haven't had a headache since the first night. Not for 10 weeks.'

The whole room takes a breath in concert, with some exclamations of happiness, stunned amazement and congratulations. It is like they have all achieved this unbelievable feat. The therapist, composed as always, just smiles.

KEY MESSAGE

It was at that moment that Gabriel learned something – a lesson that would ultimately change his life, and the lives of others also.

How powerful the mind is, and how you can take control.

For months he had been headache free. A new life, truly.

. . . and then it happened. A faint touch of 'something' in his head – a sense – the weakest of pains. Is it real? His years of exposure, tuned in to this, told him, yes . . . it's back. There it is. It had tapped him on the shoulder. That demon.

The demon's message: *Come on. Just a couple of paracetamol tablets will do the trick. Come on. They won't take over. They don't –* because they don't work. They give way to codeine – again. The return is quick. Before he knows it, it's on – lots per day – and they aren't doing anything. So accustomed to this medicine is Gabriel, he can literally taste it before it enters his mouth – sickly, almost chemical. He only has to think about it.

Resolute that he would not fall victim to the codeine or the demon again, nor join the medical roundabout once more, Gabriel walked to his local chemist, where this medication was, at the time, freely available in any quantity to anyone, and bought a packet of codeine.

He threw it, unopened, into a bin.

It took three days, but the demon backed off, slowly, and finally retreated to wherever demons go, and so did the headaches.

Gone.

So began years of this ritual. Initially every few months – the timeframes in between slowly increasing – the tap on the shoulder (as he puts it) would appear. The purchase of the codeine; the ceremonial throwing of the unopened packet into the bin; the three days; the relief; the success.

IT IS UP TO HIM

Around a decade later, Gabriel now in his 30s, and while the time between 'cycles' was now significantly longer, he had has cause to visit his doctor – a different one, as Gabriel has moved cities. While there he asks the doctor 'out of interest' if taking a lot of codeine is dangerous. 'Highly dangerous,' he says. He remembers the look on the doctor's face to this day, and his own reaction. 'The trouble is,' he went on, 'once I find out, it's usually too late. The damage is done,' and the doctor looks straight at him.

Somehow the doctor knows. Gabriel is sure of it. Gabriel has experienced this immediate reaction just once or twice in his life. His body tenses all over in less than a second, his muscles seeming to instantly spasm, his feet feel like they have filled with blood as it runs to them, he goes cold, and he knows the doctor can see shock on his face, unable to be concealed.

No further words are said.

Gabriel knows then that he could always succumb. It is up to him to prove to himself that he won't.

> Gabriel knows then that he could always succumb. It is up to him to prove to himself that he won't.

He hasn't.

CHAPTER 16

JOSEPHINE: HER PRINCIPLES AT WORK

RELEASING THE TIGER . . .

'I'm just not doing it. I don't care what it takes. This is just wrong.'

The truth is, she's scared, as much as anyone would be when taking on someone higher up the corporate ladder, especially a well-connected someone.

Presented with a task she sees as unethical, against corporate values and policies, and that would result in a reduction in standards, the job set by a more senior, heavily networked manager, she stands her ground. Josephine says, 'No,' at great personal and professional cost, much to the chagrin of the manager and to the surprise of the small throng of likeminded few, too fearful to stand up and be counted lest they too fall victim to the wrath and power of the organisational chart. Moreover, she would be left holding the baby if it all came crumbling down. Her manager is full of self-interest and does not have the same integrity. No matter how the issue is explained, this manager is determined to not listen; she wants to 'win'.

Josephine? Historically, she's been a little naive to 'organisational chart climbers' and their commitment to catapulting themselves over others, to hold others back to prevent them from shining, all in the name of self-promotion. Oh, don't tell Josephine she's 'strong'. She doesn't want to hear that. It makes her feel exposed and vulnerable. For many years, she wore a mask, as most of us do. In her case, it was also a shield, a safeguard – self-protection. The real Josephine however has been dormant, wanting to surface but not having the personal support to be her true self. The best thing she now has is her partner – her voice of reason as she describes him – though he can't completely protect her from this circumstance. He can, though, be strong. He's her emotional fuel. She needs that.

Others look at her as a potential leader but that's the last thing she wants. She finds that thought abhorrent. There is a real risk though for the Josephines of the world. Others can and do load the gun for them to fire, and they do just that to Josephine.

Though frightened and stressed by this ordeal, her wisdom – her street wisdom – is now growing not daily, but hourly. She's starting to see through those who tell her they are standing up for her when in fact they're deeply entrenched in the self-protection racket too often evident in workplaces, and are talking *about* her, depending on present company. In the company of senior managers, they're sycophants – telling senior people what they want to hear. They of course are driven by fear – fear of job or popularity loss – but at the same time, it's so telling of their character. What must their personal lives be like? Josephine thinks they must be cowards, and not people to admire at all.

They don't realise however that they're releasing the tiger in Josephine. She's angry with them, seeing how weak they are. She's losing respect for them more and more, but not showing it.

She though needs help to cope with the massive level of stress being imposed on her *by the actions of someone else*. That's right. Another human being has created this. This is so important. It is key. Ultimately, they are just someone else with temporary power. In truth, they are weak.

We shouldn't and don't have to put others on a pedestal just because their reporting line is higher up the page. It's a falsity. Respect is earned.

KEY MESSAGES

- Power ceases at some point, when we no longer have a role or title, because those are the only reasons power exists. And when it does stop, we soon find out how much respect we've earned when we had that power. We need to realise that influence is much more potent, and can be everlasting, if we conduct ourselves admirably, long after power has gone. Be careful.

- This is key. If we don't value someone else, why should we value their opinion? Sure, they may be able to cause us distress, trouble or even restrict us in the medium term, but ultimately it won't work. Are we too, someone others value? Are we earning their respect too?

There's no downplaying it: Josephine has a real problem. There's risk here for her. This really could be a threat to her career, and her reputation, regardless if she's right or wrong. The counsellor in me says this: try not to look up at these things as mountains to climb (or they can be), and instead look at them as issues to dissolve. Look down on them, not with disrespect, but for control.

Josephine just doesn't go away, but her principles take a toll on her. She faces her fears. She exhibits courage and bravery, but underneath is just as frightened of consequences as anyone else. She too has her fragility.

We can pretty much forecast the steps, including the inevitable 'investigation'. Add another huge dose of stress right there. I don't for a minute suggest that an investigation isn't required, but in so many cases these incidents shouldn't have happened in the first place. Welcome to humanness. People compete. People can also be very, very self-interested.

We may feel obliged to take a stressful path sometimes, but in doing so, it's crucial to obtain support as we traverse it. Too often we don't, and this can have consequences – big ones. Stress, sleepless nights, increased heart rate, anxiety, depression, or worse – all induced by *someone else*.

> ## We may feel obliged to take a stressful path sometimes, but in doing so, it's crucial to obtain support as we traverse it.

Josephine deserves better. She produces high-quality work, and this is often a tension point for her – the intersection of professional quality and commercial imperative – but her work really matters to her.

She is the person who earns the respect of the masses when she retires. Shallow people leave with little celebration except for a few close contacts. Ultimately, our truth is our authenticity, and the truth is that Josephine is the kind of person even the 'higher ups' secretly, and sometimes later, not-so-secretly, admire.

Who would most of us prefer to be like? There's a little bit in all of us wanting to be like Josephine I think. Courageous.

She does struggle with one question, however. Is she just a little too principled at times? That can be a very lonely place.

The end result? It's not a complete vindication of her stance. This organisation just won't do that. They cease the process against her, albeit with some wording excusing and biasing away from themselves. She's not completely happy, but is satisfied enough to cease also. She did have a tendency to attract criticism by way of her approach but is now a much more streetwise woman – and they won't take her on again.

KEY MESSAGES

- Ultimately, someone else's opinion is worth no more than the amount we value them. Sure, they may be able to affect our progress in the short term, but that is time limited . . . and being authentic is worth the wait.
- Power or authority is only temporary. Influence can be permanent.

CHAPTER 17

KATIE: THE HERO'S HERO

SHE'LL LEARN A LESSON

'Yes, I did it mum. I did it. I did it.'

No, she's not calling out with excitement as a child should. She's protecting herself, this small five or six year old. The switch, as it's called, a thin green branch, stings the back of the two innocent little legs of this beautiful girl, not much more than a toddler. Tears. Fear. Pain. She says anything to stop another hit from this cruel, out-of-control adult. Imagine it – this 'big' person, three times her size, someone she is supposed to trust above all others, screaming angrily, swinging this weapon down to cause real pain.

Oh yes, she'll learn a lesson alright, but not the one intended. In fact, she'll learn more than one.

Fast forward to her teenage years.

'What do you think you're going to achieve by this mum?,' the then 15-year-old calls out as the bedroom door is locked behind her – for the day. That's right, for the day.

Fast forward again, to her adult years.

This now mature woman has changed the world, literally.

As you can tell already, she obviously had a very tough upbringing, and it scarred her. How could it not?

Studying by dim light, she made it through high school and obtained entry to nursing studies. She made a life for herself, travelled, and met her future husband. Even as an adult, her mother attempted to damage her and poison the relationship. To a large extent, she succeeded.

They came from very different backgrounds – him from a stable, upper-middle-class family. He was not at all pretentious, but was treated as though he was – reverse snobbery in action. Their relationship was a dichotomy, with difficulty in amongst the devotion.

Her past though coloured her future which put intense pressure on the relationship. History would come back to haunt her. Embedded mistrust and suspicion – how could it not be, having been brought up in that environment. Cruelty.

Her sister passed away, too early, at 52. She found out through a social media post.

He didn't understand any of it. How could anyone be like this? His upbringing was at the other end of the spectrum. His bent was to always try to keep families together. He was a slow learner, very slow, and didn't realise until much, much later in life that sometimes it's better, and safer, to keep away.

They had beautiful children who grew up to be wonderful adults. What an achievement. She spent her life ensuring that they did not have the same upbringing she did.

When her children became young adults, she took them back to meet her mother – just once. As they drove out of that town, they thanked her for saving them.

Katie is an excellent employee, incredibly well regarded wherever she works; loyal, polite, tolerant, pleasant. She doesn't suffer fools lightly, and that includes managers. You would never know it though. She wouldn't say anything. Needless to say, she doesn't think much of false or shallow people.

These days, she appreciates everything she has and takes nothing for granted.

> These days, she appreciates everything she has and takes nothing for granted.

KEY MESSAGE

We just don't know who we are working with or what their background is.

Katie changed the world. She broke the link. She was the catalyst. She changed the direction of her children's lives, and so for their children, forever.

She changed the world, and people don't know.

If ever anyone deserved an Order of Australia, it's Katie.

CHAPTER 18

THE VERY BEST OF HUMAN NATURE

THE TSUNAMI

It is 11 March 2011. Unsuspecting people were simply going about their daily lives; me going about mine; all of us around the world.

Where were you on that day?

I had no idea I would one day have a link to that event, albeit a very soft one, but a link nevertheless, and another awakening.

The figures vary a little, but that was to be the day some 20,000 people would lose their lives, countless more would become homeless, losing everything – everything that mattered to them. Still today, thousands are displaced.

The earthquake triggered massive walls of water, striking the northeast coast of Japan, off the coast of Honshu, at the Tohoku region. The scenes were beyond horrific. These people are you and me.

Unbeknown to me, I was to closely befriend some wonderful human beings not long after. My friends Keiko Nakahama, Naohiro Usui, and more, after the event travelled to the area to assist and be with those in need. This was a group of pilots, cabin crew, airline staff and others. I hadn't met them at this stage.

> ## KEY MESSAGE
>
> Support others to do great things. Let them be. Help them do it. You will reap the rewards more than you can imagine.

In 2012 I was in Japan to assist with the start up of an airline, observing crews going about their business, guiding and assisting where necessary. I was in the flight deck.

On one flight we flew north from Narita, enroute to Sapporo. On the return flight, around halfway, we flew over Sendai, a place that had become synonymous with the tsunami.

'Look outside,' one of the pilots said. 'You see, nothing grows. The sea water has destroyed everything.' He was right. For some kilometres inland, the land was brown; lifeless. The saltwater inundation literally stopped anything growing. It was shocking.

What a gift to be able to have a plan view of the world and see it with my own eyes. It's stark, and real. Pilots deal directly with nature every day; so too do those at sea, and on the land.

It confirmed my long-held view that we can't beat nature – shouldn't try – shouldn't want to. We should see ourselves as part of nature and work with it. Only then will we stop damaging it, and ourselves. It's why I'm also very optimistic. The change is underway, and yes, in aviation, transport and all sorts of other industries as well.

> We should see ourselves as part of nature and work with it. Only then will we stop damaging it, and ourselves.

People of all ages, all around the world, are driving this. To succeed though, we need to stop criticising what is or has been and encourage and support change. Critique it certainly, intelligently and respectfully, but immediately becoming aggressive will shut down progress, guaranteed. *To continually knock others is to build a wall to them, when they are very likely the ones who can make the major progress we need.* This is our *era*, not our generation. We are all in this together. Yes, I know too, that we can meet intransigence but we have to deal with it.

KEY MESSAGE

In my experience, it's far better to make it impossible or extremely difficult for others to say no when trying to achieve something, rather than trying to use force. The issue then is how to make it hard for them to say no. It can be done.

Looking earthward from above, it's clear to me that we need to start to build further away from our coastlines, and let nature do what it does. It will, anyway. Is it controversial? Yes. Expensive? Massively. Can we do it in a progressive, respectful manner. Of course. Does it have to happen tomorrow? In some places, yes. In others, let's just make a start.

As for this group of very special people, well they get together each year and go back to that area. They meet with those they helped. They celebrate together – that's real humanity. I have been honoured to have been invited to join them. I'm going.

Now we've met just a few of our co-workers, imagine who else we have out there? Armed with this incredible knowledge, let's see how we can best work with them, and have them work with us.

PART III

SO YOU WANT YOUR CREW TO FOLLOW YOU? HERE'S HOW.

CHAPTER 19

YOU WANT ENGAGEMENT? IT'S ALWAYS, ALWAYS IN THE 'HOW'

AND THE 'HOW' IS ALWAYS THE 'WHO' BECAUSE THE 'WHO' KNOWS 'HOW'. LEARN TO BE THE 'WHO'.

If I was to draw a coloured diagram representing engagement across most organisations, it would look something like this: imagine a triangle, representing the organisational chart (more on org charts in the next chapter). Now colour it green at the top, through to blue in the middle, becoming red at the bottom. Then imagine green flashes appearing throughout (mainly at the bottom) representing new starters; this green fading to red over the period of a year or two.

Green is great.

Blue is okay.

Red is not good.

Surely we're looking for green or at least blue for the most part. If we can't say we have that, something is very wrong, but we're not alone.

119

What can we do about it then?

Well, the very first thing is to stop spending money on 'engagement programs'. Just stop.

Let me tell you that if we don't address one thing first, the rest is pouring money down the drain. The most important, the most effective, but sometimes the hardest thing to do: we have to remove, as much as possible, those factors that degrade morale, engagement and mental health in the first place – and that is always in the manager–staff relationships. Always.

> We have to remove, as much as possible, those factors that degrade morale, engagement and mental health in the first place – and that is always in the manager–staff relationships. Always.

We can instigate as many incentive and engagement programs as we like, and they won't change anything. They might produce a very short-lived fun factor, or might work for a new hire for a very short time, but before long, the reality of the culture will surface. Moreover, if staff are already cynical, it will inflame things immeasurably. Why? Because if we give a prize or gift to a cynical person they'll think we're just trying to buy them off. Money doesn't work either. Sure, they'll work for the money, but not us. It doesn't mean they're engaged, or supporting the organisation. In any case, people become desensitised to levels of money. It also has extrinsic value only. Remove it, and the decline matches the removal.

No, if we really want engagement, look to the future. Imagine. When we're all, say, in our 70s, looking back at our careers, maybe talking to our grown-up children and our grandchildren, what will we be saying?

Sure, we'll want to have been a part of successful, profitable enterprises – but in truth, we'll be looking at what made us happy *within* our careers, the careers we chose when we were young. We want to be able to look back with pride. What were the highlights? What are the really wonderful memories? Satiate that for our staff and we're halfway there. The other half? Listen up.

Back to manager–staff relations.

How to lose your staff in an instant

There were 42 staff members in the meeting. Some came from interstate, at their own expense and in their own time, such was the intensity of feeling throughout the workforce.

The room was a typical meeting facility with tables and chairs laid out neatly. The CEO was sitting so as to be able to see everyone clearly. Attendees were very attentive. They would be. They had been in enterprise bargaining discussions for a very long time, without success. Morale was at rock bottom. They felt totally disrespected.

At the head of the table, next to the CEO, was another fellow, the person who had arranged the meeting. One of the attendees pointed to this man and said, 'He is the only one we respect,' just like that. 'He's why we're here.' The CEO did not respond, but clearly noted this internally. The fellow was a trusted mentor for the CEO. He was very well-regarded by the masses. These people simply would not show up for any of the 'roadshows' put on by other managers.

There was an agenda, however. The enterprise bargaining agreement was not going to be altered no matter what. With single-minded intent, the CEO batted away every point raised by staff, intelligently I might add. Cool as can be, without so much as a flinch, each question was dealt with fluently, even if it wasn't what the audience wanted to hear.

There was a reason given why each point was negated. Masterful. Respectful even. It could have been successful. So skilled was the CEO to this point, that one particularly vocal employee succumbed, with, 'Look, we know we're paid well but . . .'. That should have been it. Over. Worn down slowly. But then the CEO dropped in one line that destroyed any semblance of respect, an own-goal. With an unfortunately timed slight smile, he said, 'I'm on the board of Company X. I could be earning much more there than I do here.' Gone. You are talking to a bunch of people trying to get a pay rise and better work conditions and you're boasting about how much money you could easily earn elsewhere? The boss's current remuneration was also probably 10 times what the staff were earning. That was the end, not just for that meeting, but for the CEO's level of respect. Forever. It didn't seem to bother him, however.

When it was mentioned at the lunch break that it probably wasn't a good idea to talk about how much money he could earn elsewhere when this group was trying to get a pay rise, the CEO's expression went cold and hard. It was like he'd never had anyone say anything like that to him before.

What does this mean? Words really do matter, and they work.

The CEO had an agenda, and was using the trusted manager to try to influence an outcome, precisely because he had sway over the group. The manager had wanted to bring the parties together to try to reach a solution and better understanding, personalising it. It became apparent however that the CEO was using the manager's sway to try to influence the staff. This manager was not 'swayable' however. The manager's standing within the workgroup went through the roof for even trying to get the parties together. The CEO's went south, irreparably.

The CEO should have asked the manager if he would assist in the negotiations.

KEY MESSAGE

Be open. Be honest. Hidden agendas don't stay hidden. They become apparent, and will expose the real person. We know negotiations are just that. Each side will use tactics to achieve an outcome. Using tactics is one thing. Using people is quite another.

HOW TO LOSE YOUR STAFF IN A FEW HOURS

Many of us have been to numerous management conferences, but one particularly stands out in my memory for all the wrong reasons.

There were about 200 of us in the conference room, the seats set out in rows, with an aisle in the middle, leading up to the elevated stage at the front. There was management representation from right across the company in the room.

The mood as we mingled before we entered was mixed. People were happy to see others, but morale varied by department and even within departments.

In we went, and sat at our allocated seats, around eight per row, each side of the aisle.

Proceedings began with a short 'hello' from the Chief Financial Officer, and him doing his equivalent of firing a starter's gun to kick off the very first 'activity' – an ice breaker. Oh no. Apart from a very few (obviously new to this almost universally dreaded ritual), a collective pall descended over the room.

On cue, attendants walked along the rows and handed out one blank sheet of A4 paper per row.

We then all had to stand and find a place where we could form a circle, facing each other. The piece of paper was placed on the floor in the middle of the circle. Our task was to, one at a time, put our foot on the paper and introduce ourselves to the group. By the time we had all had our turn of course, eight people had a foot on the single piece of A4 paper, facing each other, obviously at very, very close range. We had smiles of a sort on our faces; smiles hiding our true feelings of humiliation and embarrassment, and thoughts of ridiculousness and childishness at the whole idea. It truly was infantile, the kind of thing you might see in a preschool, although I even have doubts about that.

That completed, we returned to our seats.

Up stepped the CFO again, this time carrying on about how much fun that was for everyone. Now the real show was about to begin.

This time he introduced himself, his title, and welcomed us all to the conference. It wasn't what he said however that grated on our nerves, but how. It seems he imagined himself as a gameshow host for the day as the more he said, the more excited he became, until he reached fever pitch, and what was obviously a pre-planned crescendo, calling out loudly, '. . . and now, with no further ado ladies and gentlemen, our Chief Executive Officer, Peter Brown !!!!' (not his real name).

With that, the CEO literally ran from the back of the room, along the centre aisle to the front, jumped up the steps to the stage and took the microphone. 'Hey, hey, hey everyone! Welcome, welcome!! It's great to be here!!' The megastar had arrived; the one we'd all been waiting for . . . Thank goodness, we're saved . . . The exuberant cheering from the few executives in the front row almost drowned out the muted clapping from the other 192 attendees.

The scene was set. No mind readers were needed. 'This is our leader . . . ?' 'Can you believe what just happened?' The best one from someone in my row was, 'If he does that again, I'm sticking my foot into the aisle so he trips over . . !' That was the best ice breaker of all.

This poor fellow proceeded to ask random questions about our company's achievements and what was going on, the reward for which was in a large bucket on the stage: chocolates, sweets. A correct answer resulted in a chocolate bar being tossed to the person with a strange sounding, high-pitched yell, 'Chockies! Chockies!', as he threw them around the room. We very nearly climbed under our seats with embarrassment for the poor fellow.

It was all well intended of course, but it didn't just *not work*; it was harmful, such was the immaturity of the performance. I felt so sorry for him. To add insult to injury, the CEO proceeded to list other business leaders he considered his heroes; those he emulated and modelled himself on. The trouble was he was nothing like them, and we knew it. How could this person be so naive?

YOU WANT OUR CUSTOMERS TO *LOVE* US?

The usual breakout group sessions were in action throughout the day, one of which centred around customer service. The facilitators summed up our public standing at the time as one whereby the public 'liked' us, but the company now wanted them to 'love' us. It was sad. The room went silent. It had the opposite effect. They were in denial. They simply did not get it. Morale was so low, and they could not understand that the general opinion within the organisation was all that mattered was the share price, and that if they wanted the public to love us *the staff had to love the company first*. It's that simple – and it was *not* going to happen.

Reconvening after lunch it was obvious there were fewer people in the conference room than there were in the morning. Some managers had left. For sure, that was a risky manoeuvre, and somewhat impolite, and it resulted in disciplinary action. Punishment.

I think their actions spoke for themselves. There was no respect. The executives needed to look in the mirror, be honest, and ask themselves what they had done to cause this.

KEY MESSAGES

- No, you don't automatically know what's good for your staff. Ask them what they want.
- Treat your staff as adults, please.
- Be a leader others aspire to be like.
- It's always, always in the 'how'.

Now let's look at how we can treat our people like people should be treated. When we give our best, we give them the best chance to give theirs.

CHAPTER 20

ORG CHARTS, ORG CHARTS . . . BUT WHAT'S THE REAL PICTURE OUT THERE?

MORE THAN JUST BOXES AND LINES

What do we see when we look at an organisational chart? Boxes. Boxes of positions. Positions for managers. Managers who are specialists in their field or role (or we think so).

Get all the right people to fill those boxes and we're on our way, right? We'll get the job done. Sure, we'll add in some training to help them. This is the structure we need to fulfill the needs of the company.

That's true. Sometimes also the positions are mandated by regulation or law. Fair enough.

Why then does it so often not work? We've got all these great people, so why are we having problems? Why are some disgruntled? We hear the lunchroom talk. Why the sarcasm; the cynicism? Why is it just, well, ordinary around here? Why is it we too often look around the office and see so many just 'doing their job', not sparking, not happy? Worse still, they're not happy but they don't leave!

What if we're not going as well as we think? We're making good profits; we're growing, but . . .

Let's have another look at that org chart. This is what *someone* has deemed is required for our company to function, right? It's a technical document; a theoretical map. It's like a spreadsheet, all neatly laid out – everyone in their places.

Sure, we need these jobs done and we need good people in those positions; no argument there. The problem that often arises is the classic org chart is more like a funnel, an upside-down funnel, and a funnel can be restrictive. It also assumes there's only one ultimate leader.

What if an organisation has the capability to achieve more? What if others didn't want to be 'leaders' but just wanted to have an effect, to *do* something. What if our organisation had the potential for much more? What if we just had more of . . . everything.

What if?

The classic org chart also induces strong competition for few (and a reducing number of) places. Some leaders see this as 'healthy competition'; friction, promoting best performance. Maybe, but if so, only in the short term. The bigger issue is that it seriously raises the potential for undesirable human traits to emerge, especially with a steeply angled org chart (an isosceles triangle). A shallow chart allows for more opportunity and far less incidence of poor attributes – especially self-interest, self-importance or egotism.

The org chart is a chart; a *chart*, nothing more. *It doesn't run the company or a department. You do.* The chart has boxes and lines. The boxes are human beings. If the boxes were gears, we would be running a car gearbox, a machine, but even then, the gearbox would *only be as good as the person who designed it*, nothing more. It's one person's, or one board's, idea of success.

We have a choice though. We can either be limited by the gears that *someone* has designed, or we can take an honest look at it and acknowledge that the boxes are people. People are not machines, and we simply must maximise their potential. Not only that, but they have to work together. It's a company. A company is a group of people, working together to try to achieve something – hopefully.

> We can either be limited by the gears that *someone* has designed, or we can take an honest look at it and acknowledge that the boxes are people.

. . . but the chart also has lines.

Let's look at the lines instead. 'Reporting lines', they're called. Yes, we have to be responsible to someone. Yes, we have to complete our tasks. Others are depending on it. I do have trouble with that term though, 'reporting lines'. It certainly cements one's status, our position in the hierarchy, doesn't it? We sure know where we stand, I'll say that. It tells me that someone above has more *power* in this organisation than another; more *clout*; more *say*.

What the whole thing doesn't tell me – or you – is *what's really going on*. It's stifling. Sure, some like to have a well-defined set of tasks – procedures all laid out – but is this all we're capable of? Are people truly working with who the chart says they should be? Do they communicate well? Do they not get on? Is information being stifled (by their position description or a poor relationship)?

Would they work better with someone else? Is their PD really working? Adequate? Do they have better ideas? Oh, and these are only a few possible questions.

We need more than a survey to sort this out . . .

Done well, we can find out so much more.

KEY MESSAGE

Now we're talking about the difference between a *manager* and someone doing a *management job* – and they are two different things.

Let's look at those terms: org chart and reporting lines. The org chart may as well have been called an electrical diagram of generators (the boxes), with wires connecting them (the lines).

In the classic Org Chart, they are reporting lines, not relationship lines, and that is where our culture starts or stops, right there.

The lines are not just lines . . . or at least they shouldn't be. These are *culture* lines. These are *entrepreneurial flair* lines. These are *ideas* lines. These are *communication* lines. These are also *not necessarily those I want to mix or work with* lines.

I'll go further.

Much of the time, sadly, these are *stifling, restrictive, really ordinary* lines. These are *I'll shore up my position* lines, *keep control* lines, *not let your idea through in case you look better than me* lines, even *I don't want you to leave and find another job in case you end up with something better than me and so if you express interest in leaving, I'll treat you differently, and maybe even exclude you* lines.

KEY MESSAGE

If we turn this around, we end up with:

- *Not stifling, restrictive or ordinary*
- *I won't shore up my position*
- *I won't keep control (because I won't have to)*
- *I will let your idea live (because it will be better for me too)*
- *I want you to get a better job if it's good for you . . . lines.*

We also end up with:

- *Culture, entrepreneurial flair, ideas, communication and those I want to work with . . . lines.*

No, it's not some idyllic concept. It can be done. It just doesn't have to be. We must find out what's really going on, and what's possible. And no, it's not a survey or questionnaire.

Introducing one of my own ways of assessing and improving organisations: The Organisational Genogram. Different. But it has no downside and massive upside.

It's a strange term, for sure – genogram. It's basically a family tree of sorts, but diagrammatically representing the links between people and whether the links are strong, broken, tense or a host of other bases – ideas, collaboration, even friendships, all waiting for discovery. Again, *it's always, always in the how.* How we source this information, what information we're looking for, and most importantly, *how we're going to deal with it, and our people,* once we've found it is crucial. Be warned, the chances are very strong that we're going to find out things that we just never imagined. Are you courageous enough to find out? Are you willing to accept? Are you ready to make serious change?

Ultimately, real leaders usually transcend the Org Chart, no matter what position they hold. It may not be in the usual manner (via the very same Org Chart) but they will find a way.

Are you a leader?

Maybe we're missing the obvious. Let's have a look.

CHAPTER 21

CAN YOU READ THE SIGNS?

'DANGER. NO PEDESTRIAN ACCESS.'

The track was well worn, straight across the grass, across the dirt, through the gate (with a sign on it) that had now been propped open – obviously by someone fed up with opening and closing it – and not one person closed it. Literally hundreds of people walked this way every day.

Someone had measured the distance from the carpark to the office – 1.2 kilometres – and much of that without cover. And I counted around 20 signs – 'Danger. No Pedestrian Access.' There were bollards, tape and orange cones too.

Oh, there was another way to walk, with a bit more cover, but it was longer.

These staff members had been 'relocated' from a carpark they had been using for years, to another much, much further away, and they were insulted. The authorities could have put up 100 signs telling them not to walk directly across to their workplace and it wouldn't have done a thing. They were going to run the gauntlet no matter the

133

consequence. The truth is, who was really running the gauntlet in the end? Not these people.

I well remember my primary school principal. He had a saying, 'Listen with both eyes . . .' We didn't really understand what he was on about at the time, but I certainly do now. What was he saying? You're not listening. No, not to their words – *to their actions*. These staff are saying, *something's wrong*.

THE BIG FOUR SIGNS THAT SOMETHING IS WRONG

Staff are sending us messages all the time – 70% of communication is visual. Let's call these visual signs. Now before we go apportioning blame (and yes, we know there are those who slacken off and don't pull their weight), not everyone is wrong. Here are what I call the 'big four signs' that something is wrong in your workplace:

- **High levels of sick leave.** Endemic high levels of sick leave indicate the company has a cultural problem, or it could be that a particular section of your workforce has a cultural problem. Whatever it is, it's costing us all – you, and your staff. The very first thing we, as leaders, must do is ask what we might be doing to create this. That takes self-reflection, honesty and humility.

- **Staff working at a minimum level – just enough . . .** People leave or show up right on time. No-one wants to do overtime. No-one is happy. There are no smiles in the office. What it will produce is an increase in the number of people *who will work at just above the minimum level* to keep their position. They often don't leave their employment either.

- **Staff consistently not showing up for certain shifts.** Why would staff not want to do certain shifts? We all have our preferences, and for the most part staff will go along with those shifts they'd prefer not to do. If however there is a common thread, where you have trouble staffing particular shifts, something serious is happening. Speak to your people first. They probably have the solutions for you — *do listen to them.*

- **People reporting on each other; gossiping.** If this is happening, they've lost respect for the organisation (and self-respect too). This is one of the biggest signals of all.

Make an effort to understand their point of view. Let's not forget where we came from, for better or worse.

Of course, possibly we were never in the position of a staff member at all. Maybe we've been self-employed. Maybe we were promoted very quickly. Too often I hear comments from leaders that are clearly from someone who has never been in the position of an employee, or who has forgotten.

Now we know that for some managers the natural reaction will be to take offence, come down hard and crack down on these problems. It's costing the company serious money. We can try to stamp it out and get rid of staff members who are rorting the system. Of course, we do have some colleagues who do that. The truth is that most staff members don't want those colleagues either.

Take a breath. To begin with, say nothing. We want a result here, and losing it will make it so much worse.

> To begin with, say nothing. We want a result here, and losing it will make it so much worse.

KEY MESSAGES

- If we come down hard on everyone by introducing even stricter rules, or penalties, making life just that much more unpleasant for them all, some staff members will find another way to get back at an organisation – and then the slide has begun, often uncontrollably.
- Deal with the specific problem or people first. Taking a hardline approach for everyone is masking the problem – putting a band aid over it. The underlying cause remains. What we're likely to get is reluctant compliance – and temporary at that.

By the way, if your staff are already cynical, and if you don't want to aggravate them, stay away from using words like 'exciting new initiative', and, 'Hi team'. Most can't stand it.

Now for the elephant in the room. This elephant isn't being dealt with to anything like the extent it should be, but it can be. You can deal with it for your staff too.

136

CHAPTER 22

MENTAL HEALTH: THE ISSUE OF OUR TIME

'This could take a couple of years,' I had said to the CEO.

I was in Japan. We had been working on developing a peer support program for several years by this stage. Eventually, on gaining the trust of the local people, we succeeded – me, a Japanese psychologist friend, and some very dedicated Japanese pilots. There had been attempts by organisations and unions to establish programs before, but there had always been roadblocks and disagreements.

'How did you get it going when none of us were able to?' I have been asked many times by Japanese organisations.

The answer is trust. If there's one thing I've learned from my dear Japanese friends (I have many, and I have learned a lot from them), it's that once you gain their trust, you have also gained loyal friends for life, and I treasure them.

Mental health had not been overtly acknowledged in that part of the world. I've worked in the peer support area for some 15 years in Australia, New Zealand, Japan and Singapore. Many programs start, operate for a while, and wane. They wind down for several reasons. Often, well intentioned as an organisation might be, they forget the word 'peer' is in the title, and hand over much of the program or control to mental health professionals. That is to also forget that the very reason the groups can work so well is because it's about peers supporting peers – colleagues – those who have 'walked the walk'. Therein lies the power.

Very often though, such groups begin to focus solely on how to hold 'difficult conversations', which is important. But that is very limiting. Groups are set up essentially by selecting volunteers, training them, promoting the service, and waiting for approaches or calls. That is good, and correct. This however is more correctly peer 'response' – supportive absolutely, but it has a ceiling. It doesn't provide the scope for proactively *addressing* the mental health in the workplace issue, and the reality is we're not making the headway we need. *The problem is accelerating more quickly than we're dealing with it.*

Remember, if we're to help the Juliets, Oscars and Michaels, the first and most important step is to rid our organisations, as much as possible, of the issues that degrade mental health and wellbeing in the first place. Waiting for them to seek assistance is both inadequate and gambling. The risks are either they won't until serious harm has occurred, or they won't approach at all.

WE'RE MEASURING SUCCESS INCORRECTLY

At the executive level they will typically be wanting data – statistics – about the number of calls received and the issues being reported (deidentified, of course). This is fine, but often leads to incorrect conclusions. This assumes people will come and talk. The existence of a program is an avenue, but it doesn't guarantee people will respond.

They don't all work to anything like the extent they should. I include the aviation industry programs in this.

The key? We're measuring success incorrectly. You will know that you're winning when you have staff knocking on the door to *join a program* itself. They will do that when they find out about *what's being learned* within the program, and to do *that*, the program must be all inclusive. All staff, no matter which department they're from, should be invited to attend what I've now expanded peer support meetings to become – 'mental health seminars' – and not just the usual seminars with guest speakers. No, in the seminars I run *we talk about things that happen in workplaces every day – things that degrade mental health every day.* We confront them. We also have the movers and shakers attend, and in that room there is no status. None. The response has been extraordinary.

> We're measuring success incorrectly.
> You will know that you're winning
> when you have staff knocking on the
> door to *join a program* itself.

This is not to imply that an overarching peer support group, across the whole company, is the answer either. It isn't. The groups must be profession or department specific. Each group has its own issues, and that is another reason these programs fail – because companies don't attend to groups. If this isn't done, these employees won't feel that their issues are respected. All people are invited to the seminars, and each group then has its own session.

It works.

The real risk with data-oriented measures (numbers of calls, for instance) – and I have seen this – is that if the approaches reduce a lot, or disappear, the program is either terminated or scaled back. Executives form an incorrect view that problems have been addressed. No, it's more likely that they are being managed and the program is working.

KEY MESSAGES

- We don't need any more proof of the endemic mental health issue. It is everywhere.
- If you have reducing approaches, it means that either the program isn't set up correctly or you really have taken great strides. For the most part, it's the former. Stop paying attention to it and history will repeat itself. You'll be right back where you started.

I was wrong when I said to the CEO that our program would take a couple of years to catch on in Japan. It didn't. It accelerated in the first year and the model has now started spreading to other areas of Japan.

Oh, and I would call in to Singapore on my way back from Japan to show my wares and promote my concepts – no pushing, just offering. For some years, the answer was a polite, 'no, thank you'.

The call came one day. 'Assist us please.'

We're now operating in that part of Asia also.

CULTURAL CHANGE

If we look back at the aviation industry to the 1980s, the study of Human Factors was in its infancy, and very fundamental. For example: if the Americans build aircraft systems with switches that are operated by turning them 'on' downwards, what is the risk if we then operate a European aircraft system where 'up' is 'on'?

What happens if the message we're sending doesn't have the same meaning to the receiver? What happens if someone is not assigned to focus purely on flying the aircraft while others are sorting out a problem? (There is a well-known accident where an aircraft flew into the ground as the crew were all focused on what turned out to be a faulty light globe. The Air Traffic Controller was concerned at what he was seeing on his radar screen but also didn't communicate this concern clearly enough.)

It grew from there. The 1990s saw Human Factors become built into the way the industry (more significantly, flight crews) operated; the 'way we do business'.

The mental health issue has to do the same. It cannot be a 'bolted on' subject, and must be part of the way we all operate, no matter what industry we're in. The issue is, how do we do that? In my experience, the vast majority of executives want a mentally healthy workplace. The truth is, most don't know how to go about it, and frankly they can't be expected to know everything. The 'top' then doesn't know how to do it, but for the most part, neither does the middle or the rest.

'The culture always starts at the top' – there's truth in that of course, but it's too big a statement. It's one of those mantras again. It's not *always* the case. The culture often isn't any good because the 'top' has no idea how to set it. The 'top' needs our help. There are ways. Here's a big one, and one that I incorporate when working with organisations.

> 'The culture always starts at the top' –
> there's truth in that of course, but it's
> too big a statement.

Perfection: all leaders, or those aspiring to leadership, must spend 12 months as part of one of the groups I refered to earlier. Let's call them 'Staff Support Groups', because they are much more than peer support groups, as you can now imagine.

It is not onerous by any stretch. They will learn what's really happening on the frontline. They will learn how to deal with it. They will learn about themselves. They will learn *a lot*. They will change for the better. *They will take this culture upwards with them (and home)*. 'Cultural change from below' has now happened. Oh, and for those not predisposed to thinking this way? They *absolutely* must join a group.

A NOTE ABOUT MENTAL HEALTH ASSISTANCE

Many organisations have an EAP (employee assistance program) and that's a good thing. The issue is though that they tend to be *very* underutilised. There are reasons for this. If you want to improve the uptake rate (and get better value for your investment), the EAP counsellors must have, and be seen to have, strong links to and very good knowledge of the relevant professions. If not, staff members simply won't use them. There are ways to ensure this.

There's more to it. Sometimes staff members believe reports on individuals are provided to their employer (groupthink again). It's not true. They can't.

Staff sometimes look for a long-term link to a counsellor, and one that they will ultimately get to know. EAPs provide shorter term assistance.

I work with EAPs very differently.

EAP counsellors must be educated about the stressors attached to each profession. They must have knowledge of what each profession entails, what each does on a daily basis. They must have this knowledge *first*. The staff members must know that the counsellors know this to be encouraged to seek assistance.

To achieve this, I recommend:

1. Limiting the number of counsellors your EAP provider allocates to your organisation.
2. Educating those specific counsellors about your employees' particular professions, and common issues.
3. With their permission, listing their names on your own mental health wellbeing site (you should have one on your overall company site).
4. Advertising the fact that these people have been educated about each profession and that they can be contacted via the normal EAP number and asking for the specific person.

It works.

Now this next story just makes me feel great, and does a whole lot of good too.

CHAPTER 23

WHAT DO KOREAN SLIPPERS AND A BRITISH TV SHOW HAVE IN COMMON?

THE HALE-BOPP COMET AFFAIR

The year is 1997, and the world is again looking to the heavens. Halley's Comet had appeared in 1986. The Hale-Bopp Comet is now passing by.

People are flocking to the best locations to see this once-in-a-lifetime event. Not to be outdone, airlines are also taking advantage of their unique ability to transport comet watchers up and away from the bright lights of the towns and cities and into the clear air of the higher flight levels, where there is little dust, smoke or pollution. These 'comet flights' are operating each evening. The hope is, of course, that there's no high-level cloud, but that's the chance to be taken, and the passengers understand. Sometimes the best-laid plans don't work out, the weather doesn't play the game, and no comet is seen, but for the most part, it works. If it doesn't, I might add, a good time is had by all anyway, such is the mood, the excitement. They almost feel like explorers rather than passengers.

The event was being recorded and reported around the globe.

A film crew from the iconic UK program *Blue Peter* travelled to Australia, known to be one of the clearest locations on earth to view the comet. This particular evening, they were in our flight deck – two people, one with a video camera, the other commentating. In those days, visitors were allowed to travel 'up front', with the final approval of the Captain.

Blue Peter, if you aren't aware, is a program with a massive audience; millions.

'Should we?'

It was a successful flight, with good-quality video and polished, entertaining in-flight interviews. Towards the end of the flight, still in the flight deck, our two 'extra crew' started talking.

'Should we?' one said to the other, clearly implying that whatever they had in mind should occur; instant agreement was the response from the cameraman. 'But only one . . .' such was the clear value of the yet-to-be-revealed proposal.

Then came the explanation. They turned to us. They had approval to give a *Blue Peter* pin. So coveted was this small pin that they could not give us one each. I was the lucky one.

What I was to learn was that this was a powerful little pin. It had the ability to really open doors, for the owner was deemed to have done something very special. How humbling. I was in the right place at the right time. The pin could gain entry to all sorts of wonderful places. I've never tried, because it remains as closely cared for as my most valued possessions. It's like gold, but better.

How could a small, plastic pin be revered as it is? It doesn't gleam like a diamond or shine like a gold nugget. It can't be melted down and made into something else. It can't be cashed in (although there has been something of a black market in them, apparently).

Something else must be happening here.

The value of course is in the eyes and heart of the beholder, and the followers of *Blue Peter*. What a credit to the creators of this program and all those who have ever been linked to it that it has attained such a standing. It is a lesson.

Any organisation could have pins produced and distributed – to employees who have done something extraordinary, for example – and it wouldn't work. Why not? In most cases the horse has bolted. It needs to be put back in the pen first, and the pen rebuilt. A new 'pen' (organisation) has the opportunity to get it right from the start, however. What am I saying? I'm saying the organisation has to earn respect first. A pin is a worthless piece that will find itself in the bottom drawer otherwise. It's not possible for the pin to build that sort of loyalty. The company has to do that first. The pin then, represents – is a measure of – what the company has done. If a company can't do it, you, as a departmental leader, can at least try to do it for your staff.

So what do the *Blue Peter* pin and Korean slippers have in common?

KOREAN SLIPPERS

The organisation's culture was not conducive to high staff morale, an issue well known and, sadly, well earned by the previous management. With new owners, there was a chance to change it. I could only hope to assist the whole organisation through a demonstration of what we could do in our own department. There was no forcing it. It would only happen if they, the executives, wanted it to. Time would tell. The only option then was to focus on what I could control – my own department and anyone who engaged with it.

Parents are powerful and influential. As a parent, you are being watched even when not conscious of it. Crucially, if a child then doesn't have the full picture about something, they fill in the blanks themselves, and sometimes with the wrong outcome. Parents take note. We're on show. In my case, I was fortunate in so many respects. One of my memories is of how my parents treated their staff. They had built a notable business with a number of administrative and managerial staff.

Every time my parents would travel, and I do mean every time, whether for business or pleasure, they would bring back gifts for these staff members. The pleasure they received was only eclipsed by the joy my parents experienced giving them. I remember one morning my father stopped as he walked through the office. He turned and asked one of the long-standing employees, 'Therese, how long have you worked for us?'

'Twenty-six beautiful years, Mr Smith,' was the reply. Both smiled.

Embedded memories remain. They form us. Hopefully most are good ones.

> Embedded memories remain. They form us.
> Hopefully most are good ones.

My trips to South Korea were many, and commonly two weeks at a time. There is a place called Itaewon. It's a market, and a magnet for tourists, famous for its nightlife, restaurants and shopping.

You could pick up almost anything. On one of my early visits, I spied these colourful slippers. You could buy them by the bag full and they were anything but expensive. Now it wasn't the only gift I brought home – I brought back many – but was one of the best. Gold.

On returning to the office, I handed them out. Smiles all around. What I didn't expect though was that people would wear them – then and there. On they went. Shoes off, slippers on. I have a memory of the office staff all sitting upon a long table, having morning tea, slippers adorned.

They loved them. I could have brought back expensive things, but they wouldn't have been as treasured as those slippers. Not a chance. Had they not appreciated their work environment, those slippers would have gone into a bag, to be perhaps worn at home, or not at all. Oh, and then there were the delightfully irreverent photos I received of my staff playing up in my office while I was away on other trips – feet up on the desk – slippers in full view.

Thank you for those signs, everyone.

KEY MESSAGE

Korean slippers equals *Blue Peter* pin. Priceless.

There are some people who just cause us grief sometimes, but don't worry, they won't forever. You'll rise above all of that (and them), won't you?

CHAPTER 24

THE 'STOPPERS'

No, SYSTEMS AND POLICIES WON'T LOOK AFTER IT ALL

CEO: 'I've got this note in front of me. It says, he's been told it can't happen.' (The note is from a senior manager – a 'stopper'.)

'What do you want to do?'

Staff member: 'I want to open another staff base, and I can prove it will be beneficial for both the staff and the company.'

CEO: 'I don't have a problem with anything you have done. You've gone the right way about it, through each manager first, on the way to me. If you can open a base, with mutual benefit, and can find the staff to fill it, go ahead.'

Staff member: 'Thank you.'

We opened a new staff base in Sydney, and it worked, beautifully.

Manager: 'If I do it for you, I'll have to do it for everyone. It'll set a precedent.'

'It's right there in the policy manual. Chapter 4, paragraph 4.3.1'

'There is a roster and leave allocation system. It's right there for you to read.'

Staff member to a colleague: 'It's all we ever hear. No, no, no. The guy's a real . . . They all are. They're all the same.'

'I even spoke to the CEO at the last staff meeting. They couldn't understand the problem. "Of course we can do that," she said.'

Yes, of course it's hard. Systems actually can't be set and left to run everything, as much as we'd like them to. There are just too many variables when it comes to working with people. Sometimes we have to look at the 'system' and expand its horizons.

New manager: 'I just called to see how you're going,' feigning friendliness, naively attempting to conceal an agenda, and clearly aiming to deliver a message discussed with other managers. 'Going well? Great. Oh, I see you're looking after things in Australia, and in Asia. We'll have to have a look at that. You're only supposed to handle Australia.' The agenda? It's about power over another. Restrict their progress; prevent them shining; maintain control.

Slightly less senior, but experienced and streetwise manager: 'Oh really? That's interesting. My PD says otherwise. Have you read it? If you like, you can speak to the CEO. He's sent me a very complimentary email, offering to assist in any way he or his staff can. Would you like me to send it to you?'

New manager: 'Oh . . . no, it's okay.' The tone had changed.

Now this is too common. Forget whatever else an organisation is trying to do to build a company culture; they can make or break it single handedly. They are the 'stoppers'.

> Forget whatever else an organisation is trying to do to build a company culture; they can make or break it single handedly. They are the 'stoppers'.

Senior in position, but not quite at the top level, they have a reasonable amount of power and influence (on executives, who really don't know better), for now.

For reasons best known to them (if they're honest with themselves), certainly known to astute others, but sadly too often not even *conscious* to themselves, they will prevent things from happening.

Faced with a determined or upstanding employee (accepting that troublesome ones sometimes need a response like this), they can quickly revert to a formal reply based on and clearly worded in policy or legal speak. That's not managing. That's not leadership. That's just being a messenger, hiding behind a policy statement. That's a machine; a car gearbox.

Organisations generally consist of three parts: hardware, software, and oh, yes, people. If we don't get the 'people' part right, the rest is like a machine with no oil, and often the machine ends up seizing.

Why does it happen?

We hear a lot about emotional intelligence these days. Well to many, EI is like AI – artificial intelligence; they don't have to do the thinking. At the extreme, EI is like FI – Foreign Intelligence! It's like an incomprehensible language, making no sense at all.

Just what is this thing called EI then?

Well, search the net for a definition and we'll be flooded with answers, many of which are like this:

'The ability to identify, use, understand and manage emotions in positive ways to relieve stress, communicate effectively, empathise with others, overcome challenges and defuse conflict.'

Now ask a *staff member* what EI is and you'll likely hear something like this:

'A person gets it.'

'They get us.'

'They get what we want.'

Ask them to go further . . .

'They can relate to me.'

'They show respect for me.'

Crucially, respect now becomes mutual. Staff will work for leaders with EI. They will go above and beyond. These are the people who make change. They are the true opinion leaders; the 'significant others' in their work, and often personal lives. And here again, a person with EI will also display genuine humility. What does humility give them remember? Influence.

This is key. If they have influence, they can be an exceptional leader and huge asset to an organisation. Emotional intelligence and commercial imperatives are not mutually exclusive.

EI pays.

Why then do we not see EI everywhere?

There are a few reasons:

1. Perpetuation of the status quo.

    This is the big one. So often 'like promotes like'. There are plenty of technically or data-orientated managers and that's what the current leaders want. More of the same so they will fit in, be 'one of us'.

    The more ingrained this becomes, the greater the challenge *but the greater the reward.*

2. EI, and the benefits of emotionally intelligent leadership aren't always immediately quantifiable in dollar terms, and so often, that's what supposed leaders are judged upon purely. That's not leadership. That's salesmanship. Patience. The benefits will be there, and sooner than you think, but will

manifest themselves first in a more harmonious and respectful workplace, followed by more lasting signs. If we're in business, reduced absenteeism for one.

3. Technical roles are so often regarded as just that – technical, with no need for humanness at all. It's a big mistake. Don't fall for this one. Remember what the lines on the org chart should be.

Remember this: *from a low base, we make great change.* Whether we're rebuilding a department, a company or staff engagement, relish the opportunity. I do. And choose your mentors wisely.

I've come across three broad categories:

- If someone doesn't have much or any EI, it's likely, or at least possible, that they don't know it (that they don't have it).
- If they *do* know it (that they don't have it), they know it exists, but they probably don't understand it.
- If they do know what it is, they don't think it's necessary and have no interest in learning about it or trying to adopt it. Moreover, they may think it's complete nonsense and disregard it or anyone who advocates it. This is too common.

Stoppers are usually very low on EI, which certainly contributes to their behaviour.

There are other reasons why they do what they do. They could be status-chasers, pursuing business and social standing for all the wrong reasons. Aiming for positions is a good thing, but it has to be on the basis of wanting to achieve, to change or improve, not at the expense of others. All will be revealed later in life if it's for the wrong reasons.

They could be feeling intimidated or threatened by others, fearful that someone else will progress past them.

They could be trying to impress those still more senior to them, in order to try to obtain a promotion.

They could simply be unhappy people – and unhappy for others.

There are then those with genetic socialisation disorders, who don't seem to have any blood in their veins at all. They just don't get it.

How often I've witnessed it. The executives who are bigger thinkers respond positively, and just want others to get on and do it, only for a lid to be put on it, unbeknown to them. Tragedy.

KEY MESSAGES

- Staff members can find another way to get back at an organisation if we continually negate, ignore or dictate – and often we won't know it's happening, but it will cost.
- The vast majority are truly good people. Remember that. Deal with the few who aren't.
- Don't be afraid. Be the bigger thinker.
- At least try to learn about EI. It will change your life.

Now here are a few more things we really need to rid our organisation of.

CHAPTER 25

COMMON CULTURE CRUSHERS

There are few things that destroy a corporate culture as well as these.

TRYING TO MAKE A 'TEAM' WHEN THERE ISN'T ONE

'I just delete them.'

How often have I heard that? Lots. Staff won't tell you though that they're deleting them.

What are they deleting? Falsity – falsity in the form of emails that start with, 'Hi team,' when in fact they don't feel part of a team at all. *That is what they are really deleting – the emotion*, a negative one. They just don't want to hear it, read it or feel it.

We cannot force a team. There may be circumstances when a so-called 'team' has to be, such as with sporting teams. There are times when we have to work together, such as in a crew. There are times when we call them teams but they're really not. They are teams in name only. The word is a platitude.

The worst situation is when management is trying to create a team by calling it one. To intelligent people, they will see it as immature and insulting. So often, staff are just 'teamed out'.

155

There is a big difference between a 'business' team and a team to which people have a sense of belonging and committment, but achieve it and there is no downside and a huge upside.

Please, ensure you have a real team before you call it one. Build a community, the ultimate team.

> Please, ensure you have a real team before you call it one. Build a community, the ultimate team.

THE 10% SOLUTION

This approach nearly always fails.

A new guard arrives. The business isn't going well. A quick turn-around is necessary; even critical. A (nominal) 10% staff cut across the board is instituted without truly understanding the medium-term consequences, or for that matter, how the business or department operates or how it came to be in the position it's in.

In the short term of course, some good results can be made to happen as costs reduce, and the share price may rise. It often only lasts a couple of years however, and then quality drops. Morale declines, along with productivity. When that happens, it's very hard to recover.

Now this isn't to say cuts aren't required. They very often are but they need to be targeted with extreme care, and enacted transparently. Face the music, personally, and listen, honestly. It can be rough, but don't think you have all the answers.

Remember the old adage: 90% of the quality is in the last 10%. Be careful cutting the 10%.

Oh, and be extremely careful about discarding experience. There's no substitute. These are the 'go to' people; the ones who make companies tick. They know why we're in the position we're in. Lose them and we'll end up right back where we started.

RUMOURS

These are potentially *very* dangerous, both for corporate culture and, more seriously, for the individuals involved, including managers.

Address rumours immediately. To do this, to even be aware of them, there is no alternative but to be in there with your staff. On becoming aware of them, there's often a natural tendency to blame. Avoid this. Ask and correct. Do so in front of everyone, not just a few. It is virtually impossible for people to walk out of a staff meeting and, with credibility, further spread rumours *if the manager actually works with the staff.*

The amazing thing is that when someone is confronted with the fact that they're spreading rumours, they usually express distaste for those who do it, so either they don't realise they're doing it or they're denying it. Why would anyone spread rumours at all? For some, it's habitual, and normal. Others use rumours as a weapon to damage people or an organisation deliberately. Perhaps they're bitter. Then there are those who are simply mischievous.

What is very common, however, is the person who does it to be 'accepted'. These are very sad cases. They think that others want to hear these things and that it will make them popular. They want to belong to a particular group.

BREAKING CONFIDENTIALITY

How does this happen? It can be as simple as a facial expression.

'How's Tina going with her training?' The response was simply a raising of the eyebrows. Immediately, confidentiality is gone, and potentially along with it, Tina's reputation.

This is both immoral and unprofessional (not to mention any potential legal ramifications). Does the person need to know how Tina is going? Why? Do they have the right to know? Will it harm or benefit Tina?

Of course, it also happens when people talk inappropriately.

MESSAGE

Beware of those who talk about others in a derogatory manner. They are 'talkers'. If they're talking about others, they're probably talking about you too.

GROUPTHINK

What is it? As the name implies, it's about broadly held views. These views though are often irrational and are sometimes destructive. People will often hold them due to a desire for acceptance or to conform. It's a stereotyped view: 'Managers of this company are all the same. They have no idea what's going on. They couldn't care less.'

Furthermore, though, there is often an intolerance of those who don't conform to the consensus view, and at times the response to those people can be quite aggressive. This happens often in significant industrial disputes. We will commonly find people appointing themselves to address others who don't conform – to pull them back into the pack. At the extreme, groups lose perspective and hold an unquestioned belief that they are morally right, along with developing a sense of invulnerability – strength in belonging to the group. They have just entered the danger zone. Individuals lose control and lives can start to fall apart right then and there.

How then do we combat groupthink?

Let me preface this by saying that if it's entrenched, and if cynicism is rife, things may not change initially. Keep going. Don't stop. It can change.

Success can also depend on individuals. Are they strong enough to go against the crowd? Are there enough of them? Support them.

It is vitally important nevertheless to confront groupthink overtly, consistently and constantly. It can take time.

> It is vitally important nevertheless to confront groupthink overtly, consistently and constantly. It can take time.

Remember these few points – they are important:

- Confront issues openly. Don't shy away.
- Provide the facts. This still doesn't guarantee change. People still find it difficult to stand out of the crowd.
- Do encourage open dialogue. Do encourage expression of opinion.
- Be there. Be available for anyone to speak to.
- A leader must have respect to be influential. Do you have respect? Respect will empower a dissenter to disagree with the masses.

I admire the way many Japanese companies conduct their meetings. They will allow the most junior to speak and provide their views first. They will then work upwards in seniority or status. This way, staff members aren't afraid to differ with a view expressed by a more senior person.

ICE BREAKERS

Please no. Ditch them. Most people just detest them.

Just introduce people.

TRIANGULATION

This happens all the time, both in our personal and professional lives, and it's incredibly destructive.

Triangulation is unnecessarily involving a third party in a problem – such as a colleague or a manager, a relative or a friend – and it invariably inflames an issue. It's like throwing a hand grenade into the conflict. Once it's happened, it can be very difficult, if not impossible, to negate. Often the third party holds their own biases or agendas, and it inevitably leads to a worsening of the situation.

Make a start today. Remove these and watch the results.

Much of what we deal with in leadership roles relates to people. They are people just like you and me, and of all sorts. Believe me, working with people is not straightforward. Trying to pigeonhole them and manage them all the same doesn't work. Sometimes, there's just, well, grey ... but we can learn to respect and appreciate that colour. (Look in the mirror – be honest: I'll bet you see a shade of grey.)

CHAPTER 26

THERE IS GREY, AND LOTS OF IT

ATTITUDE PLUS POWER EQUALS PERFORMANCE

From the moment pilots start their basic flying training, this is one of the most fundamental principles of all:

Attitude plus power equals performance

What it says is that if the body of the aircraft is at a certain angle, and the engine power is set at a certain level, we will maintain a certain speed. There are a few other variables but that's basically it. It's a formula of sorts, with a few more ingredients (like weight, configuration and so on, but that's not relevant here). Learn it. Stick to it. It works.

To drive a car we learn how it operates; what we have to do. There are procedures.

Accountants, surgeons, nurses, teachers, pilots – so many occupations are similar, having to learn fundamentals first. After that, things start to become much more complex.

We learn by rote first and the natural feel comes later, and then we don't have to think about what we do so mechanically or procedurally. Muscle memory takes over. Then, once we're really proficient, we have the headspace to learn more and recognise what's going on around us. In the aviation industry, it's called 'situational awareness'.

Doing things procedurally is fine, and correct. In emergency situations, there are proven procedures to follow – if the situation pans out as per 'the book'. The issue is, they very often do not.

> In emergency situations, there are proven procedures to follow – if the situation pans out as per 'the book'.

Further to that, when it comes to people, procedures aren't the be all and end all. Black-and-white procedures won't address every circumstance, *and humans don't operate like that either* . . .

Sometimes black and white is appropriate. Press a button and something happens. Total up the columns and we get an answer. It's a system, designed by someone.

What if it's not a system we're talking about, however? What if the circumstances aren't as expected? What if we've come from different backgrounds? What if our experiences are very different? What if we need someone to work with us? What if they don't think the way we do? What if . . . ?

Welcome to humanity.

Of course there is black. Of course there is white. But there is a whole lot more grey. When it comes to people however, there's an infinite amount of variation; always has been, always will be, and it will always be increasing.

Can we adapt to work with others? Can we see what has seemed impossible to see?

Our **attitude** can make us **powerful**, to obtain the best **performance** from our people. It's our **attitude** that is key here, and no-one can change that but . . . ourselves.

KEY MESSAGE

Grey is a valid colour. Grey is good. Don't be afraid of it.

TOBY

He walks, ever so solemnly, past the pews on the left-hand side of the octagonal white-brick church, silence all but for the soft squeaking of floorboards overlayed with practical, hard-wearing dark-red carpet, and the occasional creaking of a timber pew as its lodgers shift minutely. Benign colours filter through the tall stained-glass windows fitted in each wall section, at the behest of the late morning sunlight, the thick scent of church-polished timber permeating the air. Six white ceiling fans turn at a respectful cadence, on this warm summer day. The congregation waits with sombre respect. A lady brushes away a tear; a suited elderly man pats beads of sweat from his brow with his white monogrammed handkerchief, shifting uncomfortably in his seat, furtively so as to not distract from the moment, his thin grey hair giving weight to his years of relationship with the family of the deceased.

The son, Toby, ascends the two awkwardly spaced steps slowly and carefully, to the small, pragmatic pulpit, modest and very unlike the grandeur of large places of worship. There's an element of safety and comfort for him behind this structure. He can hold it. It's a physical tangibility. Frequently something of a family showman, he is demure this day, at least until now. Notes on paper in hand, he takes a breath of courage and commences.

'My father showed us many things, but above all, he showed us that there is *right* and there is *wrong*, and *that's how it is.*' His right hand, in concert with his words 'right' and 'wrong', moves up and down as he pontificates about this, clearly a fatherly feature, now ingrained in his son.

The people listen courteously. Many perhaps agree with the statement. It's simple enough, surely, to be true? Others just haven't thought it through; haven't wanted to.

At this moment particularly they are looking for solace, the son and family certainly so, and the mourners listen for clues they can take away to better live their own lives, these times reinforcing the awareness of their own mortality. This though is not a time for dissection of the message. Clearly it has had a profound effect on the son, for him to relay this belief at his father's time. This, of course, is his last opportunity to do so publicly.

An amazing number of people hold this belief: right – wrong – nothing in between. They are intractable. They then also cast the ramifications on others. For them, there is no room for nuance, nor dissonance. There is black, and there is white, and with that lies the seeds of everything from disenchantment at work to war, and all in between, unless of course we agree with them that there are only two colours.

Sequestered away, deep within, many of us question this, but we are often afraid to live or accept grey, or to take a stand on it. We don't see it as a clear position. We may be afraid of others' reactions. For the intransigent within our community, however, life is a simple proposition. How can a male prefer a male partner? How could an interracial relationship work? Of course our children should go to single-sex schools. Absolutely we should drive an expensive car and we should mix with only the wealthy. Most certainly I should be seen wearing designer clothes, or unquestionably, for that matter, I will not. You will be going to university, come what may. That is a man's role, and this a woman's.

Really?

What of the children growing up under the guidance of such a martinet; an absolute authoritarian? How can they not be powerfully, and often permanently, influenced? What will allow them to think for themselves at some stage?

Our Toby has clearly been affixed with this philosophy, espoused – no doubt with all good intentions (we hope, anyway) – by his father. That is a very difficult proposition for him to refute. Of course. Why not? He loved his father and his father returned it equally.

KEY MESSAGE

Our attitudes are pretty much locked in at childhood, and once set, only another major experience will change them.

Take for example (and this happens *a lot*) the person who spends all their time making money, and buying houses, cars and material things, only to become sick, very sick, maybe in their 40s or 50s. Immediately those cars become worthless, valueless, meaningless. They then take another step, and *resent* those 'objects' for what they represent, and that's waste – wasted time, which could have been spent with family and friends, or on experiences, and those things that can never be taken away.

So it can be with relationships. Time and time again, problems occur when they needn't. It's not only the old who can be set in their ways. Our minds, and our thoughts, are very susceptible to influence at young – and not so young – ages.

How often I see wonderful people needlessly experiencing these troubles:

- differing expectations of what a relationship should be
- managing financial arrangements
- disagreement on how to raise children; their schooling; their friends
- unwillingness to accept another's view
- different upbringing such as amount of alcohol in the home, traditions, tidiness, friends
- emotional and other abuse
- repetitive and habitual arguments about the same things
- different value sets
- religious views, from strong faith to atheism
- non-acceptance of different kinds of relationships
- workload sharing
- bringing a bad experience from a previous relationship to a new one.

KEY MESSAGE

What, in your view, is the world's biggest problem today?

Ask others this question. Remain quiet as they respond.

Please do this. It doesn't matter what they say. Take note of your own reaction to their view.

What emotion does it elicit in you, if any? Does it make you upset? Angry? Happy?

Could you still work with this person? Would you still respect them?

What if they said the world's biggest problem was the dog barking next door?

Would that devalue them in your eyes?

Would you still acknowledge their contribution in an important project?

If the answer is no, or if you have negative emotions about their answers, it may be time to seek some assistance yourself. It doesn't mean you're wrong. Maybe though you need some help to deal with it.

Ask me what I think is the world's biggest problem and I'll tell you. It's argument. Useless, needless, damaging arguing. It's everywhere. It stops things happening – big things, like addressing poverty, wars, climate change.

Just think for a minute. There are sliding doors. We could have met different people in our lives just by taking another path. That doesn't mean we would have been any more or any less happy. Every relationship really is a different cake mix. There is no one perfect model, and thank goodness.

KEY MESSAGE

There is grey, and beautiful shades.

Now let's give them real meaning to get out of bed and come to work.

CHAPTER 27

THE REAL KEY

THE GOLD. LET YOUR STAFF TAKE MORAL OWNERSHIP

'He's never been spoken to like that.'

There were four brothers, all of equal standing in their very large company. They owned it, this huge enterprise.

We were overnighting in Townsville, and speaking all things business over dinner. We were talking staff retention, and the costs associated with staff turnover. We agreed there were three broad categories they dealt with in their business:

1. People who would stay long term.
2. People who would stay short term.
3. People who would stay for a while, leave and come back (drifters).

The biggest group? Group three. They would recruit them again commensurate with them being well-regarded. Sometimes they would leave again as well. The costs though were significant.

The conversation was evolving: mature, with gratifying business self-reflection evident. These leaders were rising with it, clearly warming to the limitless thinking around the table; honestly questioning, 'Why would they leave?'

'It's a sense of belonging,' I said. 'They need that.'

Quietness. I had touched on one of those subjects people in business often shy away from.

'We want to be the Qantas of our industry,' stated one. What a fantastic thing to say. What though did he mean by that? It was, at that time, that they wanted to grow their business to be not only huge, but iconic. It takes more than money to do that.

It takes loyalty. It's not about money. There are small, iconic businesses.

'We want the staff to work for the cause,' he said. Red flags were now flying in front of me. How often had I heard that? This was a key moment, and a possible turning point. Here lay an opportunity for learning for this already incredibly successful band of brothers. It had to be handled judiciously, however. So often, leaders assume everyone else will be as motivated as them.

I tread carefully, not wanting to overstep, preferring others discover answers for themselves. I don't have them all. No-one does. I was pretty sure about this one though. The conversation continued. Remember, ask, don't tell, and we'll all learn.

'Great, so what is the "cause"? Why would they do it? What's in it for them? Why should they? They don't own the business . . .' A key statement. A trigger. The penny is about to drop.

Wait right there.

They may not *own* the business, but surely we want them *to feel as though they did*, genuinely?

Giving share ownership to staff 'sort of' works, but not really.

The key? Moral ownership. They need to feel like it's theirs, that they care for it, that they're proud of it, that they want their children to work for it.

How?

KEY MESSAGE

We don't lose control of our business by allowing staff to take moral ownership. We do, in fact, gain further control and influence. Staff will listen to us; respect us.

TO DO THIS, WE HAVE TO CREATE A COMMUNITY – A WORK COMMUNITY

We hear a lot about 'teams' these days. To be frank, and as I've mentioned before, so many people are just 'teamed out'. We need to create *communities*. A community is the ultimate team. A community is genuine. A community is safe. We belong to communities. A community means we can have a go at something, and if it doesn't work, the community will still be there waiting for us no matter what. A community builds resilience.

> We need to create *communities*.
> A community is the ultimate team.
> A community is genuine.

Around that dinner table, my aim was to send signals as we spoke, referring to it as '*our* company'. They weren't used to that. There was risk in it. They could have taken offence ('it's not *your* company at all . . . '). Thankfully, it worked. It will only work, however, if said with decency and maturity, and if the listener respects the speaker. If not, be prepared to be shut down. Words are powerful.

We started celebrating achievements, but not only celebrating achievements by staff members but by the leaders, right in there with the frontline staff. No, it's not egotistical or unequal. It's showing we're all in this together, come what may.

The same ideology applies to departments within companies. Run them the same way. It works. Even if your own staff don't regard the overall organisation well, they will respect you. They will work for you. They will be loyal to you – if they feel they belong.

Remember this. When we're all, say, in our 70s, we'll want to have been a part of a profitable enterprise for sure, but what we'll really be wanting to talk about to our children and grandchildren are all the really wonderful experiences we had *in our own careers* within the company or industry as we went along.

Satiate that, and you're on your way.

. . . and remember . . .

CHAPTER 28

WHATEVER YOU DO, LET THEM HAVE FUN

THE BOX OF PRAWNS

It was a real 'era', when aircraft were designed with built-in stairs. Later they were removed to reduce aircraft weight and maintenance requirements.

The Boeing 727 was one such aircraft, with ventral stairs that extended from underneath the rear of the fuselage. Access to the stairs was through a door at the end of the aircraft cabin, and the stairs were operated by the cabin crew. The cabin, inside the door, was pressurised. Outside the door, it was not. Outside then, it was cold in flight; very cold, colder than a refrigerator. Typically in flight it would be something like minus 50 degrees centigrade or less – perfect for keeping things frozen, like a five-kilo box of prawns from an overnight in Darwin. Too easy – just sit them on the stairs and retract the stairs up into the closed position! Someone else came up with that fabulous idea, not me. It worked like a treat. The only risk?

Arrange for someone (trustworthy) to catch them when we pull up at the next airport and lower the stairs – or they could go missing . . .

Ice creams and the CEO

'Chris, I've had a report. What's this all about?' I had received a call from the CEO.

The flights ran Melbourne – Adelaide – Alice Springs – Darwin, with the reverse the next day.

It was a tradition that the First Officer would buy the whole crew ice creams in Alice Springs on the way north. We would then buy them a beer or two that night in Darwin.

This is not as easy as it sounds. Alice Springs is hot. The aircraft was parked out on the tarmac (there were no aerobridges), so it was quite a walk across to the terminal. There was also a total of nine crew, including the six cabin crew. It was quite a feat to get ice creams back to the aircraft without them completely melting.

One particular day we were running a bit behind schedule. Nevertheless, the tradition was sacrosanct. It would also not delay the next flight. We could complete all our tasks in the same time. So it was that the FO raced over, bought the ice creams and hurriedly brought them back. We all continued setting the aircraft up for the next flight.

The local airport manager clearly had no sense of humour or fun at all. On-time performance is an important factor in customer satisfaction I know, but I knew full well that it wouldn't add to the delay. Besides, I was confident I could handle any blowback from a passenger. What I didn't count on was blowback from a fellow staff member, and a manager at that.

I was accused of delaying the flight by having ice creams bought for the crew. Oh dear. Tragic. The world will stop spinning.

I was accused of delaying the flight by having ice creams bought for the crew. Oh dear. Tragic. The world will stop spinning.

I also didn't count on someone reporting me behind my back.

Back to that phone call. Now this CEO wasn't the most popular. He had a 'reputation'. I had never had a problem with him at all, however.

'Chris, I've had a report. What's this all about?'

I told him of the tradition and what happened.

His response? 'Ah, forget it. Have a good day.'

I really wonder what his thoughts were about the airport manager . . .

'I WANT TO PLAY WITH THE PASSENGERS'

It's a 6 am flight. The Cabin Manager is my dear friend Eddie, and she is the best. Bright, fun, genuine, just so great.

The TVs in the aircraft weren't working this day. Yes, there was a time before in-seat entertainment, when TV screens would fold down from the ceiling above the passengers' heads. In fact, there used to be just one or two large TV screens for the entire cabin and we all just watched whatever was selected for us. It's okay. We all survived without an endless selection. It was like going to the movies, and the passengers were all in it together. I also remember times when we misjudged the length of the movie and found that it hadn't finished by the time we pulled up at the terminal. The passengers wouldn't get off the aircraft until the movie finished!

I digress. Back to Eddie.

'Chris, I want to play with the passengers.' Now Eddie is very difficult to say no to. Who would want to anyway? She's such a lovely person. ' . . . and I want you to help me.'

'It's really early, Eddie!'

'Okay . . . ,' she said. I just knew this wasn't the end of it.

It's 9 am and the next flight.

'Chris, I want to play with the passengers.' How fantastic is this lady? It was always going to happen.

'Okay, what are we going to do, Ed?'

'We're going to run a quiz. I'll write the questions. You'll ask them over the PA. They will press their call buttons and we'll give out a few bottles of wine to the winners.'

'Okay.'

If anyone could pull this off, it's Eddie, and only Eddie.

She handed me the list of questions. Now this lady is seriously bright. I couldn't have answered half of them, truly. I was also given the instructions – the ground rules of the quiz – that I had to explain to the passengers. 'Eddie's rules.'

This was a three flight crew operation. There was no safety issue at all.

Quiz ground rules established; we began. I asked the first few questions. I left the flight deck door open so we could see the action. (It could have remained closed but we had the ability to open it in those days and I wanted to watch as best I could.)

Then, into the flight deck ran Eddie. 'Stop, Chris. Stop the game!'

'What's wrong, Ed?'

175

'You're going to have to tell them to keep their hands down. It's not fair. Some are cheating by having their hands already on the button. Not everyone can reach up that quickly!'

'You're going to have to discipline them and tell them to keep their hands away from the button'

Maximum tact employed, I politely ask these *paying passengers* to keep their hands down . . .

Restarting, all we could see was a sea of hands flying up to the call buttons as soon as I asked the questions. A few bottles handed out to the winners. These passengers would all come back. The crew would never forget it. Such fun – so 'Eddie'! Thank you, my friend.

NOSE WHEEL ROULETTE

It really doesn't take much – just a piece of chalk, a hat, torn bits of paper with names, and cheap prizes.

These days drawing chalk lines around the nose wheel tyre may not go down too well in certain countries or circles, so we just used the tyre manufacturer's letters marked on the tyres. On stopping, we check the wheel. Whichever crew member holds the paper with the letter at the bottom of the wheel wins the (very cheap) prize.

It is possible to cheat, if the ground crew know about it and I tell them which letter I want to be at the bottom. Slowly, slowly, stop *now*.

Perish the thought.

Some of the old fun needs to be brought back. It costs nothing.

Now, we all make mistakes. Sometimes there are ramifications and sometimes there aren't. We'll make more. Sometimes, also, we're the only ones who know we've made a mistake. When we do, let's not flog ourselves forever, or others for that matter.

CHAPTER 29

WHAT'S WORSE – GETTING IT WRONG, OR THE *RAMIFICATIONS* OF GETTING IT WRONG?

'STOP THE SIM. I HAVE TO GET OUT.'

Ask many pilots if they'd prefer an engine failure in the aircraft or in the simulator and they'll tell you it's in the aircraft. Why? Well it actually depends on the regime, and the person conducting the assessment (the Check Captain – an aviation examiner).

Simulators are an excellent device for training and assessing pilots. These days they impeccably replicate how an aircraft performs, and can reproduce infinite scenarios which, if designed well and conducted in the right manner by the right person, are invaluable for developing high flight crew operational standards.

In the wrong hands, they can also crush people. They can be mentally lethal, and erode standards.

'Stop the sim. I have to get out.'

This pilot was beside himself, incredibly stressed; distressed.

We stopped the simulator, lowered the bridge, and he stepped out. (There is a walkway that, when the simulator is in operation, folds up and away from the simulator, allowing it to move as required, providing motion for various manoeuvres.)

There was nothing wrong with the way this pilot had been performing. He was though suffering severely from a sense of threat that had pervaded that company at the time – threat of failure; threat of an 'interview' as a result of not passing an assessment; threat of retraining; threat of a loss of face; threat of a loss of career.

'They have to be able to perform in an emergency,' I've heard over the years from some of those managing those departments within airlines (and of course the public as well). True enough, yes, but there's a difference. A threatening environment stops the simulation being a standards test and it becomes a pressure test – the wrong kind. They can handle the various emergencies alright. It's the ramifications of making even the most basic of errors that can be the 'test', and by errors, I mean as small as using a slightly incorrect term; one sometimes of no consequence.

> A threatening environment stops the
> simulation being a standards test
> and it becomes a pressure test –
> the wrong kind.

The benefit of conducting procedures in simulators of course is that they can be done without real-time jeopardy. There won't be an accident.

Another benefit? There are no recorders in the simulators. In the aircraft, there is no escape. Virtually everything is recorded, from conversations in the flight deck, and between the flight deck and Air Traffic Control, to the countless system parameters, switching and flight path information.

How many workplaces, or staff members, are subject to that, every minute of the workday?

Some would contend that maybe there should be recorders in the simulators, which would remove any subjectivity – the examiner's judgement verses the pilot's. It's an endless argument. Personally, I don't favour it at all. Get the assessment culture right and it's simply not needed.

Our pilot on this occasion previously had some unfortunate experiences with a couple of examiners. It took some serious work, not to build up his standards (which didn't need building), but to rebuild his trust in the system. There was nothing wrong with him. He was, and is, a very good pilot. I'd fly with him anywhere.

KEY MESSAGE

If one of your staff makes an error, is it the actual result of the error, or the *penalty* for making the error, that's the real problem? Have a good think about that first and foremost.

The future. It seems such a long time away, but this is your time. The future starts *today*, and it's fantastic. Set your stage. Put on your own show. Give us all something to remember – something wonderful for us all.

PART IV

HOW DO YOU WANT YOUR 'FLIGHTS' TO BE REMEMBERED? IT'LL BE YOUR LEGACY.

CHAPTER 30

POWER OR AUTHORITY VS INFLUENCE

AND THE WINNER IS . . .

She walked through the office. Heads went down behind the dividers, eyes surreptitiously looked up from computer screens and telephones. There was an air of implied threat – ultimately threat to employment, and all that follows – family, career. It's fear.

No-one dared to do more than raise a smile. A smile is safe, and maybe even job-sustaining. Maybe it's even a little sycophantic. *The manager will like me. I should try to please her.* Laughter was a step too far though. It equals not working, doesn't it?

Let's remember something. Let's think about those leaders – I mean the true *leaders* – who generate massive respect, incredible loyalty and a seemingly endless following. Notice too that they keep that stature long after they have left 'office'. They could still open doors to the most important people in the country or across the globe. Think Mahatma Gandhi; Fred Hollows.

That's largely because of this: they didn't chase power. That was simply a by-product. They were (or are) the sort of person who didn't chase money, or probably ask what the pay was for a particular position. The financial reward, if there is one (there isn't always), just comes. Power or authority on its own is only something that comes with a title or role. It's temporary. Now influence – well, that's something different, and it can be permanent. We'll soon find out how good a job we've done when in a position where we no longer have the title.

> Power or authority on its own is only something that comes with a title or role.

KEY MESSAGES

- Under 'normal' circumstances, the normal hierarchy remains in control. In emergency situations, the specialist, the skilled or the knowledgeable reign. It could be the person with earth-moving equipment who can remove rubble from a collapsed house following an earthquake. Not even the Prime Minister can better that. Who has the 'power' now?

- If we haven't earned respect or treated people well, I can tell you, after we've left a role or retired, people won't give us the time of day when we walk past them in the street. Don't be offended. Don't be surprised. We will have earned that lack of respect. We're no longer a threat to others. Oh yes, and those who have influence and emotional intelligence will have a lot of people at their farewell when they leave a position or retire. They have the respect of the masses. Those without will celebrate with the few around them.

The very fact that the next chapter even exists speaks for itself, I think.

CHAPTER 31

WHAT'S OUR *REAL* RELATIONSHIP WITH OUR STAFF?

Memo: All cakes must be approved by the CEO

They walk through the downstairs office enroute to the stairs leading to the executive offices – the Managing Director and part owner of the company, the accountant, and the Head of Human Resources.

It's quite an expansive area down here, with people working hard for and with each other. The effort is crucial. This company – which I work for – is on its knees.

Through the incredible and endless work of half a dozen key managers, they have managed to stave off company shut down (they were given 30 days), gain the trust and respect of the Civil Aviation Safety Authority, earn the faith of a major airline based in the Pacific region to give the company a contract to introduce a particular airline aircraft to their operation – a contract effectively ensuring the very existence of our company at the time – all while tolerating a dreadful corporate culture.

This group is tight. They worked together. They did not compete. They respected each other. They sought the views of each other, even if someone was not in their area of expertise. They constantly met regulatory deadlines.

Why would I not include them in meetings – meetings which management of other carriers would never entertain? They earned my absolute respect and admiration. They deserved my total and overt support. The least I could do was ensure they were looked after as they worked.

At times we would bring along morning tea – cakes, sandwiches, snacks. Very occasionally I would approach our administration person for $20 from petty cash to buy a cake.

Back to the trio walking through our office area ... the moment they entered the area, it was as though the staff sensed a presence, and not a pleasant one – a threatening one. The lightness disappeared. Any fun ceased. A pall descended over the entire downstairs workplace. Fear prevailed. Must lightness equal not working? Heaven forbid.

As soon as the three ascended the stairs, the clouds parted.

KEY MESSAGES

- Working together, when two people are trying to achieve the same thing, one plus one is much more than two. Working separately, it can end up equalling less than one.
- Treat your staff as you would like to be treated yourself, with respect. In the end, you're an employee also.

One particular Friday, as we were working another massively long day, I ordered some pizzas to be delivered – bought myself – and a cake – bought from petty cash.

. . . and then it came. The memo. 'All cakes must be approved by the CEO.'

Really? We were unsure whether to laugh or not. Childishness and cowardice on display. For goodness' sake, if things are that tight, there are bigger problems, and if really necessary, a phone call or chat, 'We're watching every dollar right now', is the way to go. Hiding behind an infantile email like that – well, it's not going to do much for managerial respect.

Furthermore, it was suggested I move to an office upstairs. Clearly I was thought to be a poor influence on the staff, and not much work was going on. Thank you very much but I would prefer to stay 'on the frontline', with my managers and staff. I actually suggested they move downstairs instead, and really get to know how the organisation worked (and their managers, for that matter).

It didn't happen. Of course.

From then, we bought our own cakes.

I knew right at that moment that this organisation did not match my workplace philosophy. We parted ways a year later.

So many of the issues I help clients with encompass their work life, or often their specific workplace. There is often a common pattern, and it goes like this.

> So many of the issues I help clients with encompass their work life, or often their specific workplace.

Businesses often operate very predictably, and in many ways they're not unlike our personal relationships. As they grow, they change, as do our relationships.

The initial years at a start-up company, or when we start a new job, can be very exciting. Because of that, the newness, we usually have high morale. It's pretty much automatic. There is a lot of enthusiasm, and staff are happy to help out, often at any cost, for the benefit of all; for the 'cause'. They'll arrive early, stay late, work on the weekend.

When we start a new relationship, we experience something similar, a utopia. Our new partner can do no wrong. We are very self-sacrificing. We'll pick up after them (well, mostly). The rose-coloured glasses are well and truly in place. 'No-one leaves their clothes on the floor quite as nicely as my partner . . .'. Some people become addicted to this euphoric stage, and want to experience it over and over. They chase it. Of course, the end result can be a lifetime of loneliness. It's just not realistic.

After a while, maybe a year or so, we become a little tired of coming in to work an hour early or staying back late to 'get things done'. We also may become a little weary of picking up those clothes.

The honeymoon wanes. That's okay. It should. It's a natural progression. Don't despair.

We start to become a little more focused on ourselves; a little more circumspect. 'What's in it for me?' 'Why am I spending so much of my personal time working?'

At home, the newness can mask some realities – personality traits for instance, or attitudes that may not sit comfortably with us. Perhaps we're starting to realise we're a bit different. That in itself isn't necessarily a problem, but it could be. As a result of those traits, behaviours may then emerge.

A POTENTIAL BREEDING GROUND FOR PERSONNEL PROBLEMS

Back at the business, the true culture of an organisation emerges. How deep and strong is it, really? If it disappoints, we have a potential breeding ground for personnel problems, dissatisfaction, rumours and much more. This can also result in a strong sense of entitlement by the staff as their disappointment grows exponentially. Mix together lots of people, some emotions, different personalities and a dash or two of rumour material and we're out of the starting blocks with a rush. Once it starts, it's like a train – very, very hard to stop and turn around. Typically then, as engagement surveys tell the story of decline, management embarks on so-called engagement programs, and spend a lot of money and time so doing. It's usually pointless. Any effect is temporary, and a cover up, be it all well-intended, ultimately revealed. Prizes don't work. If we give a prize to an already cynical person, they will just think we're trying to buy them off. Money doesn't work. Sure, they'll work for money. That doesn't mean they're really working for us, or our company, and people become desensitised to higher levels of remuneration anyway.

At home, the risk is that the shine comes off the relationship, but often unnecessarily. We need to work through those differences and truly learn about them, and ourselves.

We really do have to allow ourselves to get to know each other, and well. Sometimes, relationships should have remained just good friendships, lasting ones. The same applies in business. For a lasting relationship, executives get to know your staff and allow the staff to get to know the real you.

It's true, we can have (or should have) a lot more control over our private lives than our work environment. We have to accept what we can influence and what we can't. A corporate culture may be something we just can't alter. It may not be for us, yet we often try to change it, over and over, at our own cost. I know. I've done it.

The leaders may not want to change.

KEY MESSAGES

- Know what's happening on the frontline. Get in there with them sometimes.
- Trust them. Let them do their jobs. They are the specialists.
- . . . and cakes help, but we can't buy staff morale. It's not for sale.
- And if you want to truly bury any semblance of respect for management, put out immature memos.

We have a choice. We can be upstanding, or . . .

CHAPTER 32

HOW DO YOU WANT TO BE REMEMBERED?

LIKE THIS?
'Now scam it'

Silence ... then, 'What was that?', we said almost in unison, incredulous as we all were.

It was time to rewrite the workplace agreement for cabin crew for this fledgling airline.

Done. Rebuilt. Presented to the Managing Director.

'That's good, yep,' he said, with a cunning, supercilious grin on his face.

'Now scam it.' Silence in the office. Disbelief. 'Make them think they're getting more than they really are.'

There was stunned confusion on our own faces.

Imagine what that did to the level of respect we had for him – gone. Below zero. Oblivion. Forever.

Some just don't place much value on the opinions or feelings of others. There are those too who scoff at the very concept of thinking about it. They tend to be the ones who just have no blood in their veins at all. Some have genetic socialisation disorders. They don't feel pain (emotional) or hurt, the way most of us do, or take offence at anything at all. If they don't feel that pain, then they don't understand it. If they don't understand it, it's nothing for them to dish it out, to inflict it upon others. They operate like a machine. It seems impossible to scratch the surface. I'm sure we can all recognise managers and leaders like this, and the effect it has on a workplace.

'With an attitude like that, they'll send the company broke,' I sometimes hear. Well yes, that can happen. They at times make a lot of money too. Such can be the brutality of business.

'You know we can't do that'

It was November. A regional airline was absolutely relying on us to deliver an aircraft for them. They needed it by February. They were planning on it, taking bookings. It takes months and months to introduce an aircraft, train people to operate it, adjust company manuals, have it accepted by the national regulatory authority and complete a whole host of other tasks.

'Absolutely,' was the 'guarantee' by the Managing Director.

There was an obvious air of doubt surrounding the customer, confirmed by a suspicious look on his face, as he listened to the assurance from the MD. Still, he took him at his word. Before I could get a word out, the meeting was terminated.

The customer left.

'You know we can't do that,' the MD said the second the door was closed.

'No, we can't,' I replied.

He knew from that point onwards, it would be me who would be dealing with the customer.

I could not become embroiled in the deceit. I don't want to become it. While I had no control over the delivery dates, I could work with the customer to temper their expectations and maintain their trust in those who would be working with them. After all, the customer was intelligent. He could see through the MD.

KEY MESSAGE

I can hear my father now. 'Never promise something you can't deliver. Tell them it will take whatever time. Negotiate. Keep the faith with them.'

'I get others to do my dirty work for me'

'We have an account here to be paid. If we don't pay it, they won't allow us to use their facilities. If we can't use those, our staff won't remain current and they won't be able to work, legally,' I advised.

The service provider was in the US, and I had a good relationship with the representative.

We were in my office, downstairs. (Remember the downstairs office in the chapter 'What's our *real* relationship with our staff?', where those who were, in effect, ensuring the company's very right to operate at all were working?)

'I get other people to do my dirty work for me, and that's you,' the manager said. 'You tell them to get f@*$ed. And I want you to use those words. I'm going to sit here while you do it.' He spoke like the classic schoolyard bully, with a look of challenge on his face – the very same seen in schoolyards in fact. Some people just don't mature.

My response: 'I won't do it.'

This was my reputation on the line now, and I wasn't about to allow someone else to destroy it. That's what bullies, right up to dictators, rely on. Fear. Fear, so that others surround them, ensuring they aren't bullied also. This group becomes their protector – for a while anyway – until the (often tragically for others) façade collapses.

Nevertheless, standing firm at the time is not comfortable.

He looked at me, and said, 'I'll never forget you said that.' Of course, I knew we were in financial difficulty, but that's not how to handle these things. It's just not. That was never going to get me to help. I could have.

I left about a year later.

KEY MESSAGES

- Sometimes we have to bend, but we don't have to break. No-one has the right to override our values. Adjust them with experience and learning if you want (and we all do), but you're in control.
- The fastest way for us to lose the respect of others is to not respect ourselves.
- Oh, and never criticise the opposition. Just point out why you think your product or service is better. If we do speak badly of others, a thinking listener will put us in the list of those who talk about others, and if we're on that list, they'll also know we could be talking about them the same way. Resist any temptation to go there. They may well come back to us.

OR LIKE THIS?

The customer is not *always* right 1: defend when you must

'I have a passenger who is really complaining about his allocated seat', said the Purser. She came to the flight deck, exasperated. This fellow was being difficult, to put it mildly.

In front of him, a lady with her young child were seated. The child was sitting in a window seat. This fellow had a centre seat.

He complained, saying he should have the window seat occupied by the child. I know, it doesn't make sense already, does it. He was implying that he, as an adult, should have preference. The issue is, this family had paid for the seat.

He just didn't let up. After much going forwards and backwards I said I would meet this person in the galley. These were the days when we could and would do that.

The three of us met. I heard him out. I reminded him that the child was occupying a paid seat. It was their right to have that allocated. His complaints were far and wide and in amongst it he told us he was a VIP and had travelled from Darwin to Adelaide 50 times and he would complain to the CEO. That's a lot of travel, for certain. I said we would have a manager meet the aircraft on arrival for him. Something just wasn't adding up however but we couldn't put it together at this stage.

Then it started – complaints about the Purser. She was standing right there. I attempted to explain to the fellow that managing 200 people in a confined place is not easy. Everyone has their own needs and wants. I also said that I had worked with this Purser many times and had never seen her anything but professional.

'Thank you, Chris,' she said, quietly. What came next was unbelievable.

Looking at me with a snide, smart smile on his face, he said, 'You know what women are like at certain times of the month mate'. Silence from the Purser and me. It was the most disgraceful of comments. The man was beneath common decency.

That was it. At that moment, the man ceased to be a valued customer, just a passenger.

'Mr Jones [not his real name], that was totally uncalled for. I'm going to ask you to go back to your allocated seat and remain there until we land. We will sort this out on the ground.'

We had the aircraft met alright, but not just by airport management, but police as well.

On arrival, the police came on first. The recognised him instantly. 'Off you come Bill [not his real name] . . .'. Then they told us he was a well-known conman and scammer. His '50 trips' occurred alright – 50 trips on scam compensation claims.

No company needs customers like this, ever.

By the way, it's commonplace for one airline with a troublesome passenger to inform the other airlines. They won't carry them either.

KEY MESSAGE

Make your decision now.

What do we value? Our decision will guide how we lead.

The customer is not *always* right 2: defend when you must

'What did she call you?' I asked the crew member to repeat what was said.

The cabin crew member was at the gate, checking the tickets and welcoming the passengers on board. This particular passenger was with a young child. They had too much baggage to be carried on with them and it had to be checked in.

'You're just a f@*$#!,' the passenger said, right in front of her young boy.

'Thank you for telling me,' I said to the crew member. 'She's not travelling on this flight.'

I felt sorry for the young child. Firstly, they would have to wait for another flight. Secondly, he heard his mother speaking in that fashion. Third, this was the example being set for him on how to deal with others.

There's no way my crew are going to be spoken to in that manner. No way on earth.

Do we want to retire with the respect of the masses, or just a handful of those around us? It's something very few think about, I know, yet it's vital, and life changing.

It may be that we're fine with the latter. Some just don't place much value in the opinions of others at all. There are those too who scoff at the very concept of thinking about it. But I hope you do.

KEY MESSAGE

Think about the legacy you want to leave, not only for a business, but for others. How do you want to be remembered by those most important to you, your family? Personally, I would like them to be proud – not just of achievements, or the amount of money in the bank, but of me as a person, how I handled myself, how I conducted myself with others, how I acknowledged errors, was honest and cared for others, and all those values most of us hold dear.

As we age, we have less and less to prove, thank goodness. We can become just plain nicer.

In earning the respect of our staff, colleagues, friends and family, we're not going to please everyone all the time. I would much rather have gained the love, affection and respect of the wonderful people I have been honoured to be with, spent my life with and worked with than anything else.

> In earning the respect of our staff, colleagues, friends and family, we're not going to please everyone all the time.

KEY MESSAGE

Be careful how you treat people. It has a real-world impact.

Good business also means doing things well.

CHAPTER 33

DO IT PROPERLY

THE BIG END OF TOWN

'So how am I going to keep you? What if the airlines offer you a job?' This was a very big businessman, not only around town but across the country. He and his family had businesses in other countries as well.

We were negotiating an employment arrangement. I was being enlisted to rebuild their aviation company, just one of their businesses. The corporate aircraft was for their own purposes fundamentally but in true business fashion, to make their assets work for them, they wanted it to be available commercially. That's good business.

A beautiful aircraft, they had bought it for a very good price and effectively rebuilt it to an immaculate standard.

Right now though, they were anything but happy with how the whole set up had been going. In fact, it had been a disaster. One of the pilots first enlisted essentially said he would fly for them only if he would be made Chief Pilot of the new company. A gun at their heads? Knowing the owners of this global enterprise, it's not a good career move.

Secondly, they had engaged one of their current staff members, actually working in another department but who had a commercial pilots licence, to establish their air operator's certificate (AOC). This had not only not gone well, but the application had been suspended by the Civil Aviation Safety Authority. This was about as bad as it gets philosophically for this company. They simply don't relate to a development like this. They value their reputation that much.

'What were you told by this person? What were you led to believe it would take to gain the AOC?' I asked the CEO.

'Six weeks and $20,000,' he said.[3]

I went silent. He read my expression. I knew what it took, and how hard it was.

'Are you sure you want to do this?' I asked, in reality putting my own potential contract at risk, but I had to be honest. I informed him that it took at least six months and probably more, and it's not the prospective operator who sets the dates, but CASA. They have to process and approve it all. It takes a lot. A lot. And it would cost much more than $20,000.

I said: 'I only know one way to do this, and that's in an airline fashion. Properly.'

'I only know one way to do this, and that's in an airline fashion. Properly.'

My other task was to train this person, the CEO, a very keen aviator who had his pilots licence, to fly his own high-performance jet.

Deal done. Agreement reached. They only change I made was to amend the contract from two years to one year. I understood the need

---

3   This was the year 2006. The costs now of course are much higher. And this figure was a large underestimation.

for a bond. Training is expensive, and mine would be in the US. I just couldn't sign up for two years, however.

Who knows? Maybe I would take another airline position. I did, later, but always remained in contact with this company, on wonderful terms and in fact did some more work to help them elsewhere.

I said to the CEO: 'I'll train you in a First Officer's role first, in the right-hand seat, and then we'll upgrade you to Captain.' This was met with just a little disquiet initially, but accepted. He soon found out why. This was no ordinary jet. French built by Dassault in 1978. Stunning performance. Very fast. The systems were of the era, and not so automated. Further pilots were recruited and procedures and manuals completely redesigned and rewritten. Training, negotiations with CASA, proving flights (this was the only aircraft of its type in the country) – we were on our way.

So went the process. So too went the costs, but up went the standards, and up went the results from CASA. The air operator's certificate was ultimately achieved and this company had its reputation restored.

The final cost? It was about six times the original figure given by the staff member. And it took around eight months, because we had to undo so much, gain the confidence of CASA and rebuild from the ground up.

I've always admired this company and the family who owns the business. The facilities were spotless. The equipment was first rate. They are very good businesspeople.

The CEO had a phrase he used a lot: 'Do it properly.'

I couldn't agree more. Cutting corners will cost a lot more ultimately, in all sorts of unexpected ways.

Oh, some years later, they sold the aircraft and the aviation business with it.

The buyers cut costs, conducted themselves unprofessionally (including in front of customers), weren't paying staff so they left (including me), and had restrictions placed on them because they weren't deemed experienced enough to operate an aircraft like this.

They went broke.

KEY MESSAGE

Do it properly.

In amongst it, don't forget your priorities, especially for those who truly matter.

CHAPTER 34

THE BIGGEST COST OF ALL

IT DOESN'T BECOME OBVIOUS UNTIL WE STOP

The airline industry is like some others – tough – tough for companies; tough for employees. The unbelievable highs and corresponding lows can and do play havoc with us, especially those of us who look for promotion, which is driven directly by growth. To take advantage of that growth when it comes, it's so often necessary to relocate. With families to consider, this is hard.

> The airline industry is like some others –
> tough – tough for companies;
> tough for employees.

Then comes the alternative – commute from another city, usually interstate, and sometimes in other countries, often at our own cost.

The airline lifestyle (and others, such as the military) is 'abnormal' in any case – overnights away and permanent shift work are not a great combination, but we still love the life. To add extra by being away even more is a very great risk. To become used to it is potentially disastrous for any relationship, because we've then *become used to an abnormal lifestyle* – yet some people do it for years.

It's not always avoidable of course, and to be frank, it can be fun and dynamic to travel and experience all that goes with it. Young children need parents around though; for that matter, so do teenagers and older kids; not to forget partners. It's quantity and quality. This is normal.

KEY MESSAGE

The damage is being done while the absence is happening, and too often it doesn't become obvious until we stop. If we must be away, be sure there is an end point to it all.

I was walking along a city street one evening with a colleague. We were in our 20s. We walked past a homeless man. 'There's nothing you can do,' my colleague said. I reacted with, 'Yes there is. We could take him home and give him a shower and something to eat.' It took us both aback in truth – he, that I had said that, and me, that I said it but that we didn't actually do it. It seemed at that time of our lives, at our young, relatively immature age, such a massive thing to do. I think we've all changed and try to do at least what we can.

KEY MESSAGE

That person could be any one of us. We just don't know when good times can stop, or be taken from us. We need to treasure what we have, and especially those closest to us.

CHAPTER 35

YOU WANT TO CHANGE THINGS? TRY THESE

IT'S YOU. YOU CAN MAKE THE WORLD, YOUR WORLD, A BETTER PLACE, NOW. TODAY.

Would you like to make a real difference? Now? *Right now?* Would you like to feel good, make the world better for your family and your staff, and be happier yourself? Of course, deep inside most of us would. I'm going to give you a few ideas that may help you do just that. You don't have to do them all. It's just how I think. Pick a few and try them; then try others.

One. Do something kind, now. It can be saying something kind on the phone, or doing something in person. It can be something big, or small.

Two. Every interaction we have with someone else changes our relationship with them, even minutely, and even with those closest

205

to us. We want it to be better. Before sending that next text or email, before leaving a voice message, or before saying something to the next person you meet, think about something that would improve the relationship (even in business). It could be as simple as thanking them genuinely.

Three. If you want to change someone else's behaviour, or their response to you, change yours first. Let's assume you've been having either a little, or a lot, of difficulty with someone else. Maybe you know, or sense, they don't like you. Try another approach. Think about it. Be the upstanding one. Be the one to rise above it all. Whatever you do, be intelligent. Be brave. Change the way you're doing something.

> If you want to change someone else's behaviour, or their response to you, change yours first.

Four. Be humble. Humility is incredibly powerful. It doesn't mean being meek and mild, introverted, quiet or any of those things. Humble people attract others. Humility encourages others to open up to us.

Even if you know the answer to something, ask the other person for their thoughts. It shows you respect them.

Five. If someone is affecting you, it tells you more about you than them. It doesn't necessarily mean you're wrong. It may mean you've reached your limit with this person, the type of person, or the issue – or it may mean you've just reached your limit for anything right now.

Maybe you should hand over to someone else. Maybe it's time to seek assistance yourself.

Six. Look at intent. People bounce off others' words all the time. Sometimes people use words as a weapon, when they know full well that the other person didn't mean exactly what they said. Before reacting, ask yourself if the person would have meant something exactly how it came across.

Seven. If someone reacts a certain way, it's all they know. It's what they know. It's their best attempt at solving a problem. They don't know any other way. (Thank you, Paul Lyons.)

Eight. Use what I call 'the paradox'. Overtly acknowledge someone else's *right* to their view, even if it's obnoxious to you.

Doing so is the first step to them potentially agreeing with you or at least being able to work with you. They will feel at least respected by you enough to try to work through things. Who knows, they may even start to like you. This can be incredibly hard, I know. Read point 20. You can do this.

Nine. Put yourself in their position.

An organisation as seen by too many employees? They feel like mice in a cage, running in one of those wheels endlessly. The more senior mice throw treats to them (so-called incentives or engagement programs) to make them keep running, or run harder (productivity).

An organisation as seen by too many managers? A factory for maximum productivity (not the product or service). And if I give something, I can't trust that it will be returned to me. (Granted, managers can get done over too. No wonder some are cynical, but let's not tar everyone with the same brush.)

Ten. Don't mistake pessimism for realism. It's just not.

'This bloke makes me want to string myself up. I spend hours working with him every day and he just depresses me. If I say the sky is blue, he'll say it could rain. Not only that, he'll always try to better whatever I say.'

I've worked with people just like this. One said he never thinks positively, and tells his kids not to either. That way, they'll never be disappointed. His poor kids. Optimism is not naivete. Optimists make things happen. We also don't have the right to ruin someone else's day, or their one go at life for that matter.

Eleven. If we do what everyone else does, we get what everyone else gets.

That might be fine for some, and that's okay too. If that's the case, be happy. We can't complain, and we can't not be happy for others who do strive for more. They're out there trying to surf the bigger waves.

Twelve. Words really do matter. Let's not unintentionally induce difference or unnecessary conflict.

I don't talk 'generation' much any more. I speak 'era'. There's so much we hear about differences in generations. Honestly, if we do that too much, we're just *creating* difference. Sure, people think differently. There are generations. That's not the real story here, though. It doesn't matter what age we are. We could be nine or 99. We're all here right now. This is our era. We're all in this together and it affects us all. Era. Think it. Speak it. It changes things. It changes a culture.

Thirteen. Whatever we're doing, it may be academically or technically terrific, but if it doesn't do anything, if it doesn't change anything for the better, it's no good. Leave it.

Fourteen. Beware the managerial rose-coloured glasses. We're more likely than not to get the truth from your staff about our initiatives. No, we don't know what's good for them. They'll tell us. They're the best judge.

Fifteen. Accept and admit when you were wrong. Others will admire you.

Sixteen. Start traditions. They work at home. They work in the workplace too. Bring something in for your staff if you've been on a work trip. Show genuine appreciation. Hold regular meetings in the open area of the office, with morning tea, and invite anyone to attend.

Seventeen. There are procedures and rules. We know that. If our children's job is to make their bed every day, that's fine. It's good. Here's the thing though. There's a huge opportunity right here to teach them more – kindness. Go and help them make the bed occasionally. In the office? Try this. A staff member of mine, the Flight Operations Secretary, was overloaded. We had a 'Flight Operations Secretary blitz'. She became the boss for an hour. Whatever she needed, we would do. If that were making phone calls, deliveries, a cup of tea, paperwork, whatever, we would do it. You know what? It only lasted

20 minutes or so. Just the fact that we recognised her workload and stress was key. The pressure dissipated. The smiles returned, for us all.

Eighteen. Find something they can control.

If a person is undergoing something stressful – perhaps they're under investigation or having problems at home – they will probably feel they have no control. Find something, anything, no matter how small. It could be when they return to work. Maybe they want to work with someone for a while. Having no control can be dangerous. It can range from disenchantment at one end to despair or worse at the other.

Nineteen. We don't want to exacerbate a problem, even inadvertently, let alone create one, yet this happens in workplaces every day. We don't have to be looking over our shoulder, but we can't box at shadows either. We just don't know what the consequences might be. Put the human element of our organisations at the centre.

Twenty. Sometimes, the answer is there is no answer.

It's happening every day. The really big negotiators fly around the world. They know they can't fix some of the huge, entrenched problems and trouble spots. They just want to keep a lid on them and keep peace as much as they can. Sometimes, there is no answer. *The answer is we keep talking.* That is the answer. Reread point eight.

Twenty-one. Remember, the best people often make the biggest mistakes. It can happen because they're pushing the limits. Thank goodness they exist.

Remember, the best people often make the biggest mistakes.

Twenty-two. It's good to strive for more or better. It's also good to *need* less. We can be happier this way.

Twenty-three. There's not just a glass ceiling. There are lots. They often have a basis in bias – gender, academic, race – all kinds. They do no-one any good and everyone a lot of harm, especially ourselves. Look at them not as a mountain to climb, but an issue to *dissolve*. Look back and down on them. They came from somewhere in our history. Where did yours come from, truly? We have a philosophy at home: 'We know the world can knock us around sometimes. When you walk through that door, you're safe. You can put your feet up and be yourself – and there's no judging. That is against the rules.'

Twenty-four. Love what you do. Treasure it. It could be gone in an instant, literally. For pilots, it's a love of flight (or they wouldn't give everything to survive in an incredibly tough and volatile industry). If they lose it, it's like an artist not being able to paint, or a musician not being able to play music or sing. It's devastating.

Twenty-five. Remember, we're writing our legacy, every day.

Twenty-six. Above all, ask, don't tell.

You're now the executive, the board member, the owner, the head of . . . you're running the show.

You're hovering above the business, the people, looking over them. Look closely. Someone catches your eye. You see ... yourself. You're in with everyone else. You, on the ground, turn and look up at yourself. You read the expression on your own face. It says, 'How are you going to treat me now?'

PART V

IT'S TIME TO 'DROP THE MASK AND BREATHE NORMALLY'

CHAPTER 36

IT'S ALWAYS, *ALWAYS* IN THE 'HOW'

No more roadshows please . . .

You have a message to deliver, and it's not good. It doesn't matter what it is, be it reduced working hours available, disciplinary action of some sort, some staff retrenchment (please don't say 'right sizing' any more), pay cuts . . .

It happened a couple of times a year, or when a major change was about to occur, like a new workplace agreement, or changed conditions: managers would visit the workplaces, on the face of it to talk to the troops and either gauge the mood or sell the message. It's fair enough to be honest, and I do think for the most part, a genuine attempt to connect with staff. The trouble is, it didn't work, ever. It didn't work for a number of reasons. Firstly, engagement was through the floor from the outset. Secondly, there was an endemic mistrust of management overall. Thirdly, there was a mistrust of some individual managers.

Why is it that very few people show up for roadshows? Roadshows – what a term for it. We know the intent is (hopefully) honourable of course, that management is trying to meet with staff out there 'on the frontline', but that term subliminally sends the message that they're going to *tell* the staff, not *listen* to them.

If engagement is already low, there can be an air of arrogance about it too. If a particular leader (or leaders) isn't well regarded in the first place, a roadshow can be like throwing fuel on the fire. When very few show up, they are sending a very strong message.

If, of course, there is good news to deliver, then really take note of the attendance. If it's still low, the organisation has a dreadful problem.

Who will they show up for then? Well, it's only for those they admire, respect and aspire to be like. That's it. Oh, there is one other occasion – when they are very, very unhappy.

Sure, you have things you want to tell them but they're really more interested in you listening to them. Golden rule: ask, don't tell.

Golden rule: ask, don't tell.

By all means, come and visit – but let's call it simply a staff meeting. A meeting denotes something much more egalitarian and equal. A meeting indicates a somewhat more level playing field, where we can talk to each other. More than anything though, it signifies a *respectful* environment.

That's what your staff want.

KEY MESSAGE

It doesn't matter who we're talking about. It could be a staff member or at a staff meeting, a friend or even a personal relationship, we can make the world a better place right here and now by just remembering one simple principle: every time – yes, every time – we interact with someone else, even those closest to us, we change the relationship, even minutely.

REPRISE

Of course, what we want is to make the relationship *better*, no matter what. That includes, and in fact it's especially relevant, if the relationship isn't good already. If it isn't, there's an opportunity for someone to be the hero here. Someone (you) can be the upstanding one and take the step to improve it.

Next time you talk to someone, send them an email or text, or leave a message on their phone, think, 'Will what I'm about to say or write make this just that bit better?' Rise above things. Be the one others admire. It's that simple, and if you can't, don't be the one. Give it to someone who can and get some assistance yourself.

It's important to understand that very few employees of any organisation will be as committed to 'the cause' as the business owner, or us, a senior manager or executive. That's right. It's normal. If we're a manager, in charge of a new project or department, of course we'll be enthusiastic, but unless they see something tangible for them, about as much as we can expect is that they may be happy for us (if we're well regarded).

An owner especially has every right to be celebrating their business performing well. They're building something – often to ultimately sell (and that's fine too). That's the point. It's their business, not the staff's. They would do the same if they owned the place. What's going to make them excited about making a record profit this year? Truly. Why would they be celebrating it? They're happy that the business is profitable of course. We're thinking though that they should be because it means jobs, right? Sure. Think about it though. Do we really expect them to be high fiving over it? Even if we have good news to share, we can't expect our staff to be as excited as us. It will depend on the news.

Now there's a thought. If we could have the staff actually do that, wouldn't that be something? More about this in a later chapter.

KEY MESSAGE

It's always in the 'how'.

The 'how' always speaks to the 'who' because the 'who' knows 'how'.

Learn to be the 'who'.

Now for some people, this comes naturally. For many others (and I think, sadly, an increasing number) it does not. This is crucial. It can make or break a difficult situation; make or break morale and an entire corporate culture.

Here's the good news: *the message doesn't always have to change but the 'how' does.* The right person knows how to deliver difficult news. Who then is the 'right' person? Well it's the person who doesn't just deliver the message and leave; it's the one who says it with genuine empathy and honesty, the one who knows what it's like, the one who stays with the recipients even with the potential backlash, the one who rejects jargon, the one who knows how to listen . . . Yes, it could be called emotional intelligence. But here's the best news of all: *any improvement in our ability to do this is better than good. It's terrific.* Think of it this way. When we travel to a foreign country and we at least try to use their language, it's an indication that we're trying to fit in and respect the country and the people. For the most part, the locals love it, overlook our inaccuracies and admire our effort, even if we do it poorly. The same applies in our own lives, and as managers. Even if a manager has a reputation for being anything but an approachable person, if it becomes obvious that they are *trying* to change, it will be recognised. It will be noted. It will be spoken about.

There is no downside and a whole lot of upside.

Let it be you.

If you can't, you need to get some help, or at least let someone else handle it.

'There's nothing better than a good First Officer,' the Captain said to me when I was a young FO myself. He was so right.

CHAPTER 37

ACCEPT THAT SOMETIMES *YOUR* *STAFF* WILL SAVE YOU. REMEMBER THIS

A HOTEL FOR ALIENS

It was around midnight as I joined the line to pass through immigration at Ho Chi Minh City's Tan Son Nhat International Airport.

Passport handed over, I waited for any of the normal questions posed to us as airline staff or crew (either having operated a flight into the city or positioning in as a passenger), which can be particularly focused at times. They didn't come. Instead, an uneasy silence emanated from the immigration fellow behind the counter. His English was reasonable, and understandable, but when he asked his initial question, the blood ran to my feet. I could literally feel it. Where is your visa? It was supposed to have been organised on my behalf, the flight having been arranged at short notice. This was, after all, a major company I was representing.

Within minutes, multiple people were poring over my passport, the foreign language making it all so much more concerning.

That was the last I was to see of my passport for weeks.

At that time, I hadn't been to Ho Chi Minh before, let alone Vietnam. It was the middle of the night. I was tired, and had been expecting to simply find my way to the hotel as I had in unknown cities many times.

Not to be.

The next thing I knew, I was in a car with some officials, sans passport, driving through strange, busy streets. We pulled up outside a very dark, dingy building – as I was told, a 'hotel for aliens'.

Escorted through the building, I remember the dark hallways had long, loose canvas rolls covering the carpet.

My room. I entered. It was equally poorly lit. It had one small window at head height, with bars fitted, allowing only a limited view outside. 'You can move inside the building, but not outside,' I was told. The door closed behind me.

No luggage. I did retain my phone, but without a charger. I tried to sleep.

The next morning I ventured outside my room. That building was just so dark. There was another person moving down the hall. I could just see his back. Other than him, there was not a soul to be seen. The place was quiet, and musty.

It was the only time I'd sensed anything like a panic attack, knocking on the door of one without entering it. It was a loss of control of my own environment and life in a very big way. The unknown. An unknown building. An unknown city. An unknown country. No passport. No knowing what was happening or what would happen. No knowing how long. No luggage (initially at least). No leaving the building. Not being able to see my surroundings. People watching every move so we wouldn't even go close to the door. They were clearly watching for absconders. Just nothing.

Three days later, and I still don't know how the message got through, one of my colleagues came to see me. I didn't know him well. He said that our CEO, a Vietnamese national, knew the Police Chief.

This man got me out. I remain thankful for his help. Some weeks later, my passport reappeared. I've been told I have a very high tolerance level, but three months later, after being confronted with many issues – both operational and business – with odds stacked heavily against success as we know it, and that I am sure would lead to serious legal trouble in our country, I returned to Australia. It's pretty hard to reconcile, for example, that an applicant for a pilot's position could present without the required completed subjects one day (and they involve the hardest of all course work), only to reapply the very next day with passes in all of them! Or that the previous Chief Pilot was actually an accountant. I didn't need that angst. I'd done it all before – rebuilt departments.

Now by comparison, this is light on. Millions of unfortunate people around the world are in dire straits, and it's a global disgrace. What it did though was give me more insight into myself. Pilots can and do handle all sorts of unexpected and critical events, the vast majority of which are unknown to our trusting passengers. That's a good thing. There's simply no need to create concern most of the time. But, *how do I handle myself in these circumstances? I'm not in control here. I'm not in command at all. In a sense, I'm a 'passenger' now. Someone else is in command of me; someone or others much more powerful. Can I control my own emotions? Can I maintain optimism? Focus?*

Pilots can and do handle all sorts of unexpected and critical events, the vast majority of which are unknown to our trusting passengers.

KEY MESSAGES

- Learn about yourself. It's how we become better people.
- I was in someone else's hands yet another 'someone else' helped me. They will help you too, one day. Thank them.
- Help someone else, even if you don't know them well.

Not everyone will respond well or do the right thing. We know that. We have to manage them too. Don't let that affect how you look after the rest.

CHAPTER 38

KINDNESS IS STRENGTH, NOT WEAKNESS

'IT'S YOUR TURN TO USE MY CARPARK'

The carparks were graded, left to right. CEO, COO, CFO, HR, Chief Pilot, Head of Engineering, Head of IT . . . well, you get the idea.

It was all very neat and orderly. And very status oriented. The executive carparks were also undercover. To be honest, it's very nice recognition, there's no denying it, and very much appreciated.

The remaining staff found a park somewhere else in the open-air general parking area.

I was often heading overseas for two weeks, conducting simulator training for new pilots. It was an exciting time. We were starting to make some money; starting to grow. My trips away were regular, sometimes every month, and at least every second.

Two weeks is quite a stretch, especially when it becomes the standard.

It always seemed to me to be wrong and a waste to have

undercover carparks (which were closer to the entrance door by the way) not being used.

Goodness me, our staff worked hard. I developed a ritual of offering my carpark to a staff member any time I went away, and everyone was given a turn. It was no secret. They all knew their turn was coming.

Some were a little self-conscious about doing so, and others I think worried about a possible response from 'upstairs'. I reassured them that it was my decision solely and I would manage any response. This was a new concept, I knew. I was setting the culture for my department, nevertheless.

> This was a new concept, I knew.
> I was setting the culture for my
> department, nevertheless.

This system went really well for some months. Our department engagement was high. We would have a regular Monday lunchtime meeting, to which everyone was invited – and I do mean *everyone*, whether they worked in the department or not. That way, people from other areas could learn about how we did things.

One day though, on my first day back in the office after another trip, I drove into the carpark and turned towards my allotted place. To my surprise there was another car there, and not the one belonging to the staff member whose turn it was. In fact, all the carparks had moved left! Now there's a signal if ever there was one. Clearly the executives didn't agree with my view on how to treat staff. They didn't want any hint of additional benefit. They didn't want any egalitarianism. 'Give them an inch and they'll take a mile.'

And they didn't want to be outshone by someone slightly lower on the org chart. Don't worry. It's common, and all about control over others.

I elected to park in the general carpark with the rest of my staff.

KEY MESSAGES

- Be humble. Learn. None of us has all the answers. Maybe someone else has a better method of generating a good corporate culture.

- If a business owner or powerful leader simply does not want whatever culture there is to change for whatever reason, it probably won't. If you think it needs changing, maybe the organisation is not a fit for you.

- Please, if you find yourself in a position of wanting the status quo to remain (or having to deliver the message), have the courage and decency to talk to the person. Don't send childish signals.

Now it's time for real courage, to see what we're made of.

CHAPTER 39

INVOKING 'AVIATIONALE'

HAVING THE COURAGE TO FACE OURSELVES – OBLIGING US TO LISTEN

'Aviationale'. No, it's not the name of a beer. I could have chosen any title, but this reflects how I think aviation and all professions should operate. It works.

Telling people they need to listen, and ensuring that a corporate culture provides the maximum possible likelihood of it actually happening, are two different things. Policies won't do it. They're necessary of course, but they only establish an enforceable principle.

As you've probably gathered, I don't favour giving advice as such, and my belief is that it's immeasurably better to pass on experience – what works for me – and let others make up their own minds. I find it a much more successful approach and one that generates more respect. I won't therefore tell you what you should do. What I do need to do is explain to you why I do things.

Just what are we trying to achieve here then?

227

I've too often seen leaders – managers – who conduct themselves like headmasters of a strict boarding school of a bygone era. We would think that as time passes, and we know more, that these things disappear into history. Unfortunately, history has a way of repeating itself sometimes, triggered I think by commercial aggression and simply too much need for competition. Organisations are obliged to push harder and harder to remain afloat, but there is a human cost to 'low cost' anything.

> I've too often seen leaders – managers – who conduct themselves like headmasters of a strict boarding school of a bygone era.

I remember my father saying, 'If we needed more work, we'd go out and get it'. He was talking about the '60s. Times have changed. While we can't change the business environment, there are ways we can better deal with it – and this one I propose is a big one.

Try to imagine a culture that could do at least some of this . . .

- remove 'ceilings' – glass ceilings, bias ceilings, 'fear of retribution' ceilings
- release the truth
- dissolve bias
- break down barriers – generational, cultural, seniority, age
- increase managerial standing
- increase respect and conversational maturity across the board
- increase safety
- increase humility
- improve relationships – manager/staff, staff/staff (too)
- improve morale and engagement

- establish a global culture, accepting of difference, able to negotiate cultural norms, extracting the best
- introduce a form of amnesty for those wanting to change
- create an elegant impasse for those people who wish to maintain their views but, of greater importance also, wish to remain harmonious.

Asking too much? Perhaps – but maybe not.

Just what is this then? The principle is so simple. It's a word – with a meaning – a statement – a statement that can be invoked by anyone, but there are conditions.

The word 'aviationale' becomes embedded across the organisation – the statement does not have to be made, but it is this:

> I respect your position (status) but I want (need) to bring something to your attention (raise an issue). You'll have my increased respect if you consider my opinion (listen to what I have to say).

The aim is to achieve all those things listed above, and to introduce leaders and managers who lead and manage for *everyone*.

Let's think more . . .

There are three possible outcomes upon someone invoking 'aviationale':

- The recipient (the person who has received the word from someone else) agrees. It says a lot about them.
- The recipient doesn't agree. It says a whole lot *more* about them.
- The recipient agrees to receive the word but doesn't adhere to the protocol.

What might we expect when an organisation adopts this philosophy? I think this:

- Most employees or subordinates will support it strongly.
- Most managers will support it due to a genuine desire to improve staff engagement.
- Some managers will not support it due to a fear of a loss of power or status. They will disregard anything that has anything to do with an emotionally intelligent approach or is managerially developmental.
- It will become more and more accepted with exposure.

Of course, in a utopian world, none of this would be required.

Further underpinning principles:

- The statement should not be overused, or it will devalue or hold reduced effectiveness.
- Its preferred use is in situations such as those with serious concerns, such as with safety-critical matters, where there are significant staff problems or serious difficulties between people.
- There is no Catch-22 here. People are not damned if they do use it or if they don't. It is a mechanism for overcoming Catch-22. It's a safe space.

Let me provide some examples.

The circumstance: A junior person believes safety is being compromised due to cultural norms or ingrained beliefs – potentially useful in circumstances where status has prohibited questioning. Issues may be safety related or of personal respect, such as not wanting to be treated in a certain way.

Preferred response: Overcome or rise above any natural, immediate reaction to disregard. Know that this junior person is respecting you but *also wants to respect themselves.* This person is possibly very unhappy or upset internally and doesn't want to be. Know that this person is trying to be courageous, but it isn't easy. Know that this person wants to hold you in high esteem.

The circumstance: Employee to executive manager: 'I realise we are in a very competitive environment but you will genuinely obtain more from me if you listen to my (career/personal) needs.' Or, 'I know it may go against what may appear to be commercial considerations but I'd like the opportunity to demonstrate my validity. I know you may have been misled before. I'm asking you to trust my genuineness.'

Preferred response: Genuine appreciation of the person raising it; having the courage (singularly) to do so.

The circumstance. Employee unhappy with his or her manager.

Preferred response: 'I respect your position (status/higher position) but I want to talk to you about something you've done that concerns me. I don't want to be afraid to do this or feel that I may be penalised. I want to find the courage to talk to you myself and be appreciated by you for doing so. I want to be open and honest. I want to address it here. I don't want to go to another manager. My concern is genuine, and my hope is that by raising this personally you will respect me more and that our relationship may even be strengthened.'

The circumstance: Person being assessed by an assessor or trained by a trainer (known to be strict or pedantic): 'I want to raise a difficult subject without fear of offending you. I feel I'm in a difficult position as I've been told something different by another senior person.'

The circumstance. Employee finds themselves trapped and unable to address a problem they have with their own manager. They feel powerless.

These are just a few possibilities. The question then arises – what if it fails? What if the senior person can't rise above?

It could fail. If it does, we've found out the true nature and depth of our organisational culture.

It could fail. If it does, we've found out the true nature and depth of our organisational culture.

CHAPTER 40

CHANGE THE WORLD WITH THIS ONE LESSON

THE MOST BEAUTIFUL LESSON

It had pieced together beautifully, this handmade dining table. Kauri pine, so clean, almost white, predating the exquisite yellow colour that was to become its natural future once settled in for its contented life, surrounded by laughter and happiness. The scent of freshly sawn timber filled the backyard workshop.

The older man leaned over, a slight occasional twinge bearing testimony to this man's joinery past and wartime history. A sandpaper block in his right hand, he smoothly rubbed the top of the table with long broad strokes. The Kauri had not been easy to find. He remembered an old mate 'down the range' who ran a sawmill. Sure enough.

Unbeknownst to him, such was his modesty, that man revealed to his son his art; it was but one part of his legacy. Embedded, too, were the learnings for his son about his father, through conversation, the most poignant of which on that day was of the one task in which his father would no longer partake. His days of wood turning table legs were gone, ever since he witnessed a colleague's life lost when doing just that, as the table leg came adrift from the machine.

The son loved every minute. Living in a different state, he didn't see his father or mother much. Nevertheless, his parents adored their children, even though they had a little difficulty expressing it physically or verbally. It was their history; very hard at times. That was okay. The family knew that. Their intent was impeccable and that's what mattered.

Watching this man hand-sand the table, his son commented that, such is the accuracy of machines, they can make things absolutely straight and flat. He was, of course, by no means suggesting sanding mechanically.

In yet another unintended, memorable, life-changing moment, his father said, 'Yes, they can, but it's like an artist painting, a chef cooking, or a singer singing. The artist will have their own brush strokes; put *themselves* on to the canvas. A chef may create a dish of their own or tweak a recipe. The singer will sing their own version of a song with their unique voice and style. The song writer has created the music with the notes. The singer brings the notes to life and sometimes they're not exactly aligned with those of the song writer. The singer may not even be especially talented, but it's them.'

The singer will sing their own version of a song with their unique voice and style.

'It's the imperfections that make people perfect.' (Ron Smith, circa 1984)

How beautiful, this lesson.

KEY MESSAGE

Of all lessons, remember this one.

Now it's time to reveal the real you. Just who are you?

CHAPTER 41

THE KELP FOREST CLOUDS

WE BELONG HERE

I belong here. So do you. We all do. In our own kelp forest . . .

It's 3 am, south of Guam, over the western Pacific Ocean, flying south towards Papua New Guinea. We're high, at 43,000 feet. The night sky is clear. The moon shines brightly. The only sound is the quiet wind rush only pilots hear. The sound envelopes the flight deck like a blanket, the ever-so-subtle changes in volume perceptible only to those flying this magnificent creation of mankind, signalling small variations in aircraft movement through the thin air. It's a sensation that to them signifies speed, just as the instrument readings do. They don't need to feel the aircraft move to sense speed. It's innate, progressively bred through hours and hours of flying experience.

It's serene, and still. It's cold outside, very cold, but we're warm. The world is peaceful here, in this place, at this time. Removed from troubles right now, we're on top, looking down and out over the horizon. A thread of moonlight is shimmering on the dark ocean, far below. At this moment, we're citizens of the world, of a global community, more part of the earth than anywhere else or at any other time. It's not lonely.

It's where I do some real thinking, true to self. I realise then that we're all still here. Anyone who has ever lived is still here. I feel it. It's visceral, with such comfort and belonging. My sense of loss for my father calms. Here, above it all, I appreciate how intensely beautiful life is and should be for every single person, and how fortunate I am. It's not so for so many, and for no reason good enough, and I want to change at least some part of it for them, and for my children. If we're going to have families, children, we owe it to them to devote at least part of our lives to making the world a better place. We are, otherwise, just breeding children, not raising them. They didn't ask to be born.

> If we're going to have families, children, we owe it to them to devote at least part of our lives to making the world a better place.

How I wish everyone could be here.

Three hundred people are on board, together. Their cocoon that is the cabin is dark, and warm. Sleep overcomes most. A faint light shines over others who just read or choose to disappear into themselves with music or a movie. Children are curled up in a ball on their seats. Cabin crew move silently in the darkness, just so beautifully, seeming to float gently past those under their care. Be it by happenstance or deity, it matters not, for this community of travellers, as unaware as are young children, is proof proper that prejudice and judgementalism need not exist when we don't know who is sitting beside us. We cannot see the colour of their skin, the design of their apparel or their gender status. We don't know their spiritual beliefs. There is a natural politeness and respect that comes with unknowing, as we pass in the aisle. Anything else is created, and artificial. Unnecessary. Harmful. We're meeting in the darkness, coexisting peacefully right here. Calm now.

Remember this moment. Take it with you. Do good things with it. Escape from those who mistake pessimism for realism, who use negativity as an excuse to achieve nothing, change nothing, or drag others back into their small world. Let not your optimism be dimmed by others, for optimism makes bad good, and good, better.

The flight deck is dark too, the lights dimmed for night flight.

Turn, look up. Soak up the stars, simply by virtue of the angle at which our planet sits, fewer in number we see in the northern hemisphere than the southern, still there are just so, so many. The tiniest of lights, yet each so bright, looking at us as we them. Imagine what the stars must see looking at us; how envious they must be to see our beautiful blue marble that looks after us, suspended, drifting, utopian. One only. We know of no other, anywhere, anyplace. Looking closer, closer, the stars see the sleeping voyagers, silently moving around the earth this night. How the stars must wish they were like this place. There is an allure, a romance here.

Just what is this all about, I wonder? Here, while I don't truly understand, I get a sense of the beginning of comprehension, like we're all a part of this magic carpet that is the universe; ours. How calm am I now. Beatific.

The winds are benign in our little part of the galaxy. They are, around the equator. If the air was coloured, like an ocean, we would see the currents, the waves. See the clouds and you're seeing the waves. Some are but ripples on the water, with a charming name – Cirrus – barely clouds at all, but wispy ice crystals, some so wafer thin, the moonlight shines through, reflecting gentle rainbow colours. Others, mountains – but not this night.

I wonder if they'll be here tonight. I hope so. They usually are, like a trusted, good friend, waiting in the stillness. The forests. I'm looking for the forests; the forests, like underwater kelp.

As being carried out to sea in a current, we don't know until it's already happened, we're inside the forest. All around are the kelp clouds, narrow, loosely vertical white tubes, sitting upright like pawns on a chess board. The stillness and tranquillity belies the energy within them. They can be rough to fly into, and the aircraft weather radar doesn't see them. The natural world can defy human technology. The turbulence doesn't last long, maybe 20 seconds or so, long enough to surprise and disturb those onboard. We try to avoid them, weaving through the kelp visually, left and right, thankful for the moonlight. We have to. In our mind, in our being, flight this night is very high, up in the astonishingly thin air, where unprotected life for us cannot exist beyond mere seconds, yet another tap on the shoulder of the wonder of the world.

The kelp is still higher than us, bigger than us. It knows no such boundaries. We cannot fly over it. It reminds us that this is nature. It has its own rules. We can't beat it; shouldn't try. We must work with it. Learn from it. It has every right to be here and to live as it does. The kelp lives. It changes, moves, waves, grows; an unchoreographed, adagio ballet. Enter; be absorbed by the forest. It welcomes us, this enchantment of nature. As we pass, more kelp emerges from the forest's darkness bearing witness to us, as though a secret message of a 'curious being' has been relayed ahead. Eerie, beguiling, ghostly white figures, yet safe; reassuring. There is no menace here. Time, standing still, has no meaning here. Come. Be free to explore. In this place, it lives tranquilly. It doesn't understand, doesn't need to understand anything else. This is the kelp's milieu, its culture. It has no need to justify, to prove, to compete. It is above all of this. Nature is. When it does show its unspeakable power, it does so not with malevolence, but to rebalance. There is a virtue, an innocence, from which we can learn.

The kelp seems to turn to watch us as we transit so carefully and silently. It has a presence – gentle, wary, like an animal seeing a human being for the first time, yet without need. This is their environment. We're the visitor; still, they do not threaten. They have no need. They let us pass peacefully. Everything is alright. Do come back.

As mystically we entered this pure place, wiser and elegantly we leave, more learned; contented, understanding, at peace, gracefully empowered.

The sun does not just rise. In a few hours, I know I will see the earth glow; a theatre with a crimson opening, then glowing fire red and blazing yellow. The master awakes. High up here, we can see the curvature of this magnificent blue sphere, our home, and behold the electric display of the sun coming alive; infinite life-giving power, right there in front of us.

It will light up the forest as well, warming, energising, transforming it by day, and readying our nocturnal kelp clouds, for they are reborn and live at night only, in the quiet and the still, in nature's own perfect balance.

Innocent of the splendour through which they have passed, our travellers are, in truth, themselves of nature. Nature looks after nature. It asks for no thanks, this forest. It is kind.

I take home with me learnings from the forest. It does not say goodbye. It merely waits. It will be here always if we look after it, always hoping, wanting, to selflessly offer more life lessons from this natural world theatre.

There's a part of me that doesn't want to leave . . .

To some, this may simply be a night flight through clouds. To others, it's a wonder of nature, of life, seen only by a few; seeing what others don't. Those see more, allowing themselves to be authentic.

They are released, not controlled or coerced; safe to see what they want to see.

KEY MESSAGE

Find your own kelp forest.

We've all worn a mask of some kind, and different masks for different occasions. The mask may give us oxygen for that moment, but it *is* temporary. It runs out. Forget it. Be you. Not being authentic is not only exhausting but a risk to our own mental wellbeing. It's also unfair – to us, and others. Just be the best person you can.

> We've all worn a mask of some kind, and different masks for different occasions. The mask may give us oxygen for that moment, but it *is* temporary. It runs out. Forget it. Be you. Not being authentic is not only exhausting but a risk to our own mental wellbeing. It's also unfair – to us, and others. Just be the best person you can.

Let those you have responsibility for know who you really are. Let them know how you think. Make yourself real, human. Don't be afraid. Do it and watch what happens. There is no downside and huge upside.

Be humble. Humility is powerful. Make sure it's genuine. Others will see straight through us if we're not . . . and find your own kelp forest. You deserve one.

CHAPTER 42

YOU CAN DO THIS

YOU CAN CHANGE *YOUR* LIFE, THE LIFE OF *OTHERS*, AND THE *WORLD*. IN FACT, WE HAVE TO . . .

So many people talk about doing great things, but don't. They talk about changing the world, but don't. They complain but wait for someone else to do something. That's not you.

The little things are big things. Change things around you and your impact multiplies. Those around you will be inspired. They *want* to be led. They want someone they can admire and aspire to be like. This is you. It has to be. This is your start.

> Change things around you and your impact multiplies. Those around you will be inspired.

My book is not about cloning others. It's about giving you courage with wisdom, passing on experience, and finding your own commitment. Most of all, it feels good to be doing good things, meaningful things, and making the world just that bit better.

Our lives are all different cake mixes. No two are the same. You'll have your own experiences. This book is a sample of some of mine. There are many more. We don't have to go through life 're-experiencing' things others have been through. We can not only learn from the experience of others but teach it – how to deal with it. That's how we can progress, and more quickly. We want those following us to be better than us, don't we? Surely that's how we should be thinking if we're truly wanting the best for the future? Surely that's the unselfish approach? The admirable approach? We want our kids to be even better parents than us, don't we? The circumstances they'll face may be different to ours, *but we want them to be starting from a higher base.* We can do this.

Too often, it seems that even though we know more and more, we go backwards unnecessarily. No more. We know more about health than ever before, yet too many don't have access to basic health services; know a lot about our planet and its climate, yet we aren't taking enough care of it; know a lot about mental health, but we're behind; and inequality, yet we see so much.

What's stopping us? Just us, that's all. We just haven't managed to convince enough of us – yet. We will though. *You and I will.*

Through it all, incredible things are happening. Humankind has a way of being very late to the party but getting there just in time. You will have read that I prefer not to refer to generations too much, that we're *all* here right now. It's not that generations don't exist. It's that we're too often building artificial barriers and creating needless division through words and terms, and separating groups, right when we need the very opposite. The younger members of our era, and the forward thinkers of any age, are going to do things differently, and better. By the way, let's not think we haven't done so many things better than those previous to us, because we have, but if we don't for instance accept climate change (and there aren't too many now who don't), let's just want to live with cleaner air and water. Let's just see others with greater empathy, all the while being streetwise enough to know that not everyone is a good person. Let's not forget that building businesses and creating communities are not mutually exclusive. We can do this.

There will always be those who will try to stop us or pull us down. Don't worry. Have courage. They won't live the life you will.

Good things, big things, are not just for other people. They're for you too.

> Good things, big things, are not just for other people. They're for you too.

As we say in the flight deck when handing over control of the aircraft to the other pilot, 'You have control'. And you do.